THE VOICES
OF OUR NATION

THE VOICES OF OUR NATION

A Compilation of Poems

The Lost Legacy Series

Ebelechukwu Elochukwu

authorHOUSE®

AuthorHouse™ LLC
1663 Liberty Drive
Bloomington, IN 47403
www.authorhouse.com
Phone: 1-800-839-8640

Published by AuthorHouse   07/16/2013

ISBN: 978-1-4817-7284-6 (sc)
ISBN: 978-1-4817-7283-9 (hc)
ISBN: 978-1-4817-7282-2 (e)

Library of Congress Control Number: 2013911992

Unless otherwise indicated, Bible quotations are taken from The New International Version of the Bible. Copyright © 1987 by The Zondervan Corporation.

Cover Impression Design Idea: Ebelechukwu Elochukwu

CONTENTS

*Let Your Voice Be Heard: Speak up now or you will die
remaining silent forever*

*Give a Voice to Those Who Have None: To the suffering people of this
world, the only hope they have to live, survive, recover, win, succeed
or be fulfilled is you. Do something!*

*God is Present in Our Daily Life: One of the gifts God gave to the world in
the past four centuries is the United States of America and one of
the gifts you can give to God is your selfless service to others.*

 # PREFACE

When we completed our last book, "The Lost Legacy," one of my good friends in the Lord expressed his discontent with using sanitized versions of the curse word "f" in the poem I wrote in the "Excerpts from the Author's next book." I apologized for offending him, which was not intended, but as suggested by the poems, use of such words in our daily life is not good and does not honor God. Parents should help their children develop enough vocabulary to express themselves. This will help them take good advantage of our freedom of expression, press, and other fundamental rights given by God and guaranteed by our constitution without arousing negative emotions.

If you were offended too, please forgive me and help me caution those around you who believe that it is cool to disrespect one another, call each other names, and speak in such disrespectful and disgraceful tone or manner. Many have lost their decency, proper manners, and courteous relation with others. It is my hope that by your good work, they can change their ways by improving their communication skills. According to Greek Philosopher, Heraclitus of Ephesus, change is the only thing that is constant on earth. I ask for God's mercy on all of us and grace to survive lost of American dreams, stable, and secured future for our children. I thank God for His mercy by granting us the current economic recovery and national progress witnessed so far and pray for more.

I thank every one of you reading this book because you helped to put it together. Yes! I heard you wondering when you helped me, when we probably have never met.

Yeah, I know, physically; but in the spirit
We met the moment I felt your spiritual pulse
Right! Your joy, your pains, and sufferings
Because we're all interconnected with each other
Your pain is my pain
Your suffering is my suffering
Your joy is my joy
Your happiness is my happiness
Your sorrow is my sorrow
If only we can trust together
If only we can hold each other's hands
If only we can encourage and support each other.
If only we can gird ourselves
Shoulder to shoulder we can win
Our unity is our strength.

Oops! I forgot I am in preface and the poems are coming later. I encourage you to accommodate my shortcomings in this book. I am not an expert in English literature or a Poet Laureate. I just enjoy writing and talking about whatever thoughts that come through my physical and spiritual minds and hindsight, including my knowledge, research and experiences. I hope you can help me tell the story better and share it with others, of course with proper credit and untwisted.

Without giving you my original thoughts and meaning that inspired these poems, I highlight basic (general literary face-value) abstracts of the poems in the glossary pages and leave your curiosity to discover the true, relative, and real meanings of them. For instance, in the poem *The Ant Hill*, I talk about the daily life of an ant hill in the ant's colony. What is the poem talking about? It will be nice to discuss it with your friends and find out what meaning they make out of it, and see if it is the same as yours, and how many similarities and differences of opinion you discovered. Just like a game!

In the poems *The Lion's Den, The Cat and Dog, The Chameleon, Chess Game on a Chess Board, and The Elephant*, the author discuss something completely unrelated to the subjects (face-value meaning) of the poems just like *The Ant Hill*. I am sure you will figure it out. This is also true about the majority of the poems, for example, *Chickens Springing Up As they Hatch, Who I Am and What I Want in Life I Don't Know, Such Noble Profession in Which You Are Called, Spooky Sparky, My Queen, The Wasteland of Americas of Native Descents, A Land of Opportunity for Dreamers of All Nations, My People,* and *Why Are We Still So Divided.*

Everyone is free to give his or her own meaning or interpretation according to one's spirit or mind. We will like to know your own meaning or interpretation. Do not take any of the poems' literary face-value meaning only. Seek the deeply hiding core principles or else your interpretation may not be the hidden treasures of the poems—the true meaning. It will challenge you and hopefully you will enjoy them. Don't let the glossary notes fool you either. Some poems may evoke your emotions or be provocative. They are intellectual, social, leisure, recreational, and spiritual exercises and please treat them as such; nothing personal. It could be used in middle/high schools and colleges. Use of race, name or noun can be interchangeable where applicable or necessary and in no way suggest preference by the author. The author is race/gender neutral and color blind.

Many of my poems are in blank verse (unrhymed verse) and some are ballads (narrative poem). We have Ballade (three stanza of eight or ten lines). Some are Elegy, Epic, Lyric, and Sonnet. Some poems are in Canto, Stanza, and Versification. Also, some are in Cadence or Ode. We did not measure the poems in poetic Feet, Meter, or Rhyme but you will find Quatrain, Tercet, Quintet (Quintain or Cinquain), Sextet (Sexain or Sestet), Septet, Octet (Octave), Spenserian (Alexandrine), Onegin and many more. The majority are songs.

I will really be grateful if you allow this book to take some of your valuable time. If you have read any of the poems before buying this book, I hope they entertained or amused you; either way, I just want to make you happy and make your day and time reading this book worthwhile. I will be grateful if you can try my other books: *How To Win Your Trials & Your Communities, The Lost Legacy,* and many more coming soon . . .

Ebelechukwu Elochukwu

 # DEDICATION

I dedicate this book to the people of Baltimore City, Paulette Taylor-Bryant, every resident of the United States of America and above all, God the Father Almighty, the Son, Jesus Christ, and the Holy Spirit.

# ACKNOWLEDGMENTS

I am grateful to those who took time to read and critique any part of this work particularly Dr. Jane Sellman, PhD, Professor of English writing, Department of Achievement and Learning Center, University of Baltimore and Jenesta Matthews. My special regards goes to Sandra Oken for her moral support while writing this book; C. Victor Mbakpuo, Esq, for his suggestions: and all the people whose stories and lives inspired this work.

Ten percent of the net proceeds from the sale of this book will be donated to Holy Trinity Family Support Center Corporation. More information about Holy Trinity can be found @ www.holytrinitycenter.org. The 501 (3) (c) organization plans to conduct empirical research to prove the author's theories. Please donate to support our initiative to reclaim the heart of our nation, the great *United States of America*. Five million dollars is needed for the research.

PART 1

INTELLECTUALISM AND
EXCEPTIONALISM

*The critical thinking process of reasoning of one's mind
is constantly in conflict with the mind (the thoughts and
actions) of one's supernatural self.*

THE ANT COLONY

Oh! Poor ants, where did you come from?
From underground, you arose;
every ground is represented.
In this colony the queen reigns.
Our world ends right under earth;
where all of us live in peace and harmony.

Oh! God thank you, our trust comes from you.
In you we put our trust.
This colony of yours, is ours now.
Our workers built it.
Yes! From the scratch they built it;
reclaimed from the aborigines.

From whom the land wastes;
those have no use for them all.
We sent our workers after them.
They ate up all the dirt;
in their mandibles they carried it
And above the earth they deposited them.

Yeah! An anthill is built on earth.
Above the ground it stood tall.
Cast with its foundation deep down the earth,
with hollows and ridges so strong,
storehouses of foods and riches abound,
and beds of comfort for our queens and kings.

Alates! They eat, meet and breed,
in the comfort we provide,
and the work we did; our labor indeed.
Winged male and female they are,
what a worker you are; a laborer in need,
you male, you sterile ant, and you worker.

We're all squinching, bigger than we look.
We're all squirting, the content of our mandibles.
That we deposit on the earth,
while building the anthill,
the symbol of our colony,
and in a land that is now ours.

Steadily we march, burning the dirt.
Hauling and pulling, until we explode.
Not exploded, we squirt the dirt.
Fighting, yet constantly moving.
Racing, till colonization is complete.
Now, our colony is established.

THE LION'S DEN

Where are you lion, Where are you?
In your den you are? There you are!
Are you in hiding, are you resting?
The jungle is wild; wide open you left it
The beasts roam the fields, where are you?
Are you entrapped; hunter's game you've become?

Where are you lion, where are you?
With guns they hunt you; bows and arrows abounds
Pa pa pa, fian fian fian they sound
So loud and very fearful; as the jungle echoed
Moving faster than they sound, past before you hear them
Are you all dead; or were you all wounded?

Where are you lion, where are you?
Here I am; and who are you?
Why are you going about, calling me out?
Asking questions; you already know the answers
Can a rope go round my neck, or trap holds my feet?
I am the king of the beasts; the jungle is my kingdom

Where did you come from, where are you going?
Their freedom is mine; so is the liberty
They move freely, when I want them to do so
Their liberty is at my will; that I ration to them
Those who violate them, receive my justice
Jungle justice violently granted; that turns them to carcasses

Here I am, home I've come
I've seen no one; no beast around
Far off I called home, letting all know
That I am on my way; soon I'll be home
Off they had gone, into hiding they had gone
What they had done; behind me they had done

Here I am, home I've come
From patrol to patrol; watching over my territory
Protecting my borders, else my sovereignty be compromised
By one of my own kind; those seeking for my kingdom
With pretense or deceit, they could infiltrate our ranks
Unless I keep watch; trained and strong to fend them off

There I was, home I've come
Up and down I roam; perambulating about
Eyes so sharp, ears wide open
Even the wind passes not by me; my senses on alert
Fearful of my enemies, in deep voices I roared
And my enemies are scared off; they know who I am

I am the lion, what a beast I am
This is my kingdom; I am the king
My children live here, my future to become
Though very young and tender; them, I must protect
Freedom, Liberty, Justice, Rights are their names
Although naturally given to all, what a golden rule I took away

THE CAT AND DOG

Meow! Miau! Uugh! Uugh!
Uh! Carney what is wrong with you
You were just happily licking
Smouching, smooching, snuggling, and robbing
Loving and playing around your liked
Surely you marked your territory

Woof! Woof! Wow-wow! Ghoo! Ghoo!
Come on now, Jonny
I see why Carney is coiled up
With hairs standing straight
Like it's going to shoot out of its skin
And tail rising up so high

Oh! What again; always bickering
Quarrelling and fighting over nothing
The territories you're fighting over
Does not belong to both of you
They all belong to the owners; your masters
Also the properties therein; everything there is

You're accepted by the people; at their service
From the goodness of their heart they let you in
With trust they shared their life
With confidence that you will protect their interest
That you will share your lives and love
To do what is best for all and sundry

Instead you are always bickering
Quarrelling and fighting over nothing
When our house is dysfunctional
Our health is failing, our lives fallen apart
When will you get it; and represent
Understand how serious our problems are

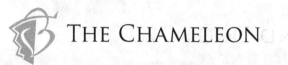

THE CHAMELEON

As I pass through the justice jungle
There was a Chameleon in the forest
His power and strength is lies
Deceit is its weapon and source
It's of authority as it moves up the tree
The more its power and authority abounds

There it was bright and blue
Then it disappeared before my eyes
It was out of sight, I thought I lost it
Then I saw something red moving
Lying flat on the bark of the tree
There it was, the Chameleon

And I thought, how is that possible
Is it the same animal or another
Maybe a member of its family
As I was pondering over this
It disappeared again; out of sight
Now I know; something is going on

Something phenomenal, something different
My eyes caught something in the air
I thought it was a fly
Then I saw the leaves shaking
Dancing around; big and green
There it was on the leaf, the Chameleon

Majestically stepping in green attire
Perfectly blended with the leaves
Could not tell them apart
For the third time, it changed its color
How is that possible; I thought again
It has to be the same lizard

As it walked further I saw another
A member of Chamaeleonidae walking away
As if running away from the former
It was green too; perfectly blending in
To the large green leaf on which they tread
Now I know, they are many; maybe a colony

A class of Reptilia, of Animalia kingdom
And it jumped off, looking like a fly
Landing on another large long leaf below
It was orange toward the trunk of the tree
But yellow towards the end of the leaf
Showing signs of the end of its life and purpose

The tree shades its leaves, as new leaves bloom
The new leaves sprout; and also blossoms of flowers
Looking back at the orange dying leaf
I could not see the Iguania; it changed again
I looked harder; there it was in orange coat
Perfectly blending with the orange leaf

It must be its nature; to change colors
As it strolled towards the yellow part
Its color started to change
Until it became yellow just like the leaf
It must be a form of protection from predators
Not just a deceit or lie to onlookers

I followed it as it crossed from one branch to another
across a pink and turquoise scarf hanging on the tree
The wind storm deposited it in plain site
It stopped, as I looked on, it changed to purple
Along the turquoise end it changed its color
Each time perfectly blending in very well

Chameleon, Chameleon what a creature you are
Chamaeleonidae, Chamaeleonidae what a world you live in
A world that is the same and changes not
But you chose to change whenever you want
To which ever color suits your purpose
You can be pink, blue, red, orange, turquoise, yellow, and green

 # THE HOLY TRINITY IS AT WORK

They always talk about the Holy Trinity
And what is that; a Church or a building?
There are three persons in one God; is that the truth?
God the father, God the Son, and God the Holy Spirit
What is the truth?
The truth is God
Who is God?
God is the word
What is the word?
The word is the sword
What is the sword?
The sword is the Holy Spirit
Who is the Holy Spirit?
The Holy Spirit is the Almighty Father
Who is the Almighty Father?
The Almighty Father is the Son
Who is the Son?
The Son is Jesus Christ

The Almighty Father became Word
The Word became flesh
In the womb of a blessed virgin
Whose name is Mary
Chosen to carry God nine months
Like every human before birth
To be like us, look like us
act like us, live like us
live with us, and have fellowship with us
To lead the way, to show the way
to teach the way, to practice the way
to coach the way, and to mentor the way
Showing that human can be like God
look like God, act like God
live like God, live with God, and have fellowship with God
lead like God, work like God, and teach like God
We can be patient, persistent, tolerant, self-controlled, and faithful
We can be humble like God; and that makes us god

Jesus Christ surrendered His life willingly
Though He is God, He humbled Himself
Never took equality with the Father
Became poor, a carpenter, and a simple man
What a humiliating and shameful death
He was tortured and hanged on the cross
Like a criminal, He was killed by us
God gave himself, His only son, to die for us
So that we may live, and have life in abundance
He made a new covenant with God the Father
For those who believe, who live like Him
Those rejected by the world, by its truth
Those that live by the truth, which is the Word
The word that was the flesh, the flesh that was the Son
The Son that is the sword, the sword that is the Spirit
The Spirit that is Holy and God the Father Almighty
Then comes the freedom and justice that is eternal
And salvation and celebration in everlasting kingdom of God

 # LOVE ON THE NOOSE

Oh my love where are you
Ever since we talked I have been hooked
Unto something bigger than any Mountain
As the conversation continued so naturally
I began to feel passion greater than life
My existence began to fizzle
Melting away every moment
Then began to flow into you
Like the Niger flowing into the Nile
The distance having no meaning
Nor effects whatsoever
to the way I feel about my one half

Yes, my love here you are
A place so beautiful, so great, and so powerful
Ever since I met you my darling
I am very intoxicated every moment
by something more controlling than any drug
Held tight by rope stronger than any metal
The diamond so dulled to cut through it
Then I found out how sick I was
The sickness found me long ago
I was dead, a moving corpse but did not know
My love so devastated beyond description
Our hearts so broken, so shattered, and irreparable

My love, I am so ill, and won't be fruitful
My sickness has taken my flowers
What is life without fruits on my tree?
You! Oh weak branches, so frail
My heart is pierced, stricken by the sword
so sharp, so heavy, and so laden
To let you go, to set you free, and to wish you well
is the honorable thing to do my love
As much as I love you, it's just, if truly I do, it's right
Yes I love you truly, please go now
Because I love you go, leave me and my God
Lest I die; to see you hurt, to feel your pains

Though you weep not, such a real man
I hear you cry, in the middle of the night
I hear you sob; and I hear you moan
All from the pains nature has brought us
In the day you smile and you cheer up
In isolation you carry your chin
You carry your jaws when there're no eyes
Because I love you and I know you're hurting
You're hurting now because I am hurting
That is why I have to let you go my love
I am healed, now everything inside is gone
Because I found love above, I will live again

BELOVED I HAVE HEARD YOU

I love you so much my beloved
and I have heard you; everything you said
I heard you, whether it is a curse, or it is not,
it is a misfortune, what a misfortune, I was to carry
Who can carry; a mountain, a plateau
filled with volcanoes, pregnant with lava
alive with consuming fire of love, destructive like flames
burning with gas, such our love encountered
oh sickness where did you come from
you tumor when did you get to her
and you cancer who is your master
that I may plead for my beloved
is it money you want or is it silver, gold, or diamond
if so I will bring it bountifully before you

That you may leave my beloved alone
If our love is not good enough
to soften your heartless body mass
What kind of body without heart have you
attacking every host body; every organ
Every cell hosting you is your target; your prey
Where is your power you sickness
That I may take it, your source I will quench
Such that you will not breathe
Your life I will take from you
Because to my betrothed, you have visited
For no reason, her life you have taken from her
Our love you have stolen, our heart you have broken
The organ you harvested, ate, or damaged

But her life, you must not touch, and cannot take
Because it belongs not to you but to her creator
From whom comes her strength; power to overcome
To set her free from your strongholds
And repair the damages you have done
Restore her hope for the future; for a fulfilling life
To be a mother without a husband or pregnancy
Give home to the orphans, adopt those without one
Because I love you my beloved, I heard you
The wedding will no longer take place
It's just, the right thing to do for our sake
The Church will not wed us even if we insist
Marriage without possibility of procreation isn't allowed
Sex without possibility of procreation isn't acceptable

Though you weep, you wail, you moan, and you cry
Day and night, morning, afternoon, and evening
Tears cover your eyes, nose dripping, eyes swollen
From the pains; suffering that gush through your gut
Spreading through your brain and to the whole body
To me, your friends, family, and to those who love you
As we share your love so also we share your sorrows
Just know that you are not alone in this journey
I am here, we are here, right here shoulder to shoulder
I will always be there, those that love you will always be there
You have won, we have won, you have conquered it all
Tumor is gone, cancer is gone, and sickness is gone
You'll no longer die, now you'll live; you did not know you'll live
If you can find, the will of God in this, you'll live a fulfilling life

WHEN THERE IS LIFE, THERE IS HOPE

I am born free, a citizen of this great nation
in liberty, justice, and boundless opportunities
with hard work, the sky is my limit
I will go to the Moon, I will touch the Sun
If only the powers that be, will let me be
Will they let me be; they are suppose to?
They should, the Constitution said so
The Lord said so; God given rights they are
Our inalienable right; inherent endowment it is
Oh God! Please let me be free, please protect me

You powers that be, you principality
you in authority whip me not, flog me no more
for I am wounded, my flesh is torn
my wound is bleeding, my heart is broken
Oh! Oh! Oh! Injustice, you inequality
Oh! Oh! Oh! My master, my lord
All I wanted is to pursue my happiness
To live my God-given life without molestation
Exercise my fundamental rights and liberty
And suffer no abuse, enjoying all appurtenances

Oh my lord, why can't you keep me safe?
From the hands of those bullies
Those cowards who chase me around
The wicked feed me with crack
And drug me to insanity; unless I run for them
From one corner to another in exchange
Drug wraps for money, less I be maimed or die
From the tools of their trade or trader
With that they shoot, they hit, and they club
Where are you the powers that be; you my masters?

Oh God Almighty, you are here with me
Rise up for me against these evils
For I am hopeful and my faith is strong
Where man had failed, you always come
Intervening and interceding for those
That have no one, those forgotten
You the people rise up with me and save yourself
For our Lord is here; our Master is
He has come for us, to save us all
From those who abuse us; who took our lives

LET'S WORK AND LET'S SHARE

He that is healthy, let's work
He that works, let's share
The joy of receiving is in giving
Greater is he that gives
Than he that receives

Am I able to do the work?
No! I can't, I am afraid I cannot
No one trained me, no one coached me
They want me to work, but who taught me
You who never worked, and you too

Not even your parents or your parents
Neither your grandparents nor yours
So why bother me now, why such demand?
That I may go and fail, like you all failed
Always sitting down at home you busy bodies

Is not you or me but them
Those who kept us home
Who sent us down the pit
A bottomless hole it is
An abyss down the bay

We were weak and couldn't crawl out
Even if we did, we couldn't find our way
Unable to navigate the waterways
jump through the traps set for us
and maneuver the nets thrown to catch us

They really meant to keep us there
By feeding us and making us weak
Somewhat and somehow comfortable
So that we'll never think where we are
Never rise to compete and conquer life

Our days may be over for we are weakened
But your days are beginning for you are strong
Where we failed you will succeed
The traps and the nets you can bypass
For our voices are stronger when we're united

That is why we demand that you should try
Because we the united stand by you
Our experiences are there to guide you through
If only you agree to try, to take a chance with faith
You will become what we are not, will never be

# THE EAGLES IN THE SKY

The eagles in the sky, how lonely you are
You are out there all by yourselves
In your world there is no other but you
From your world, you watch everyone else

With eyes so sharp and strength so vigorous
You watch over everything under you
To the left and to the right, you tilt your head
The sight of the earth so clear in your brain

As you hover from one end of the earth to another
With your wings so wide and so spread
You float from the sea to the land
Your wings flapping against the winds

You pick and choose your prey
With every caution not to be caught
As you target to make your dive
And your victim caught with your feet

Your wings so large and so strong
Waving and flapping so hard
Full of energy and abounding in powers
Bidding the earth and therein goodbye for now

Until next time you return to the land
With nothing to give in return from all your journeys
even with what the earth gives you eagles
That you may live on it; watching our movements

Where are your hearts and your fairness?
To give back to mother earth who gave you
Though it's not your fault that you're blessed
By God who made us all what we are

You are asking us where our hearts are
Always assuming we are such an unfair creature
Because God set us apart from you; so high
Do you know how we got up there, got so high?

By the benevolence of He that is high and mighty
Not only by our wings, strength and power
How can we bring more things to the land?
When you see not all the things we give to this earth

How could you see that, you envious fools?
When you are blinded by envy and jealousy
For everything we grab from your land
we gave something in return that is ours

We make the way so that you may live
By bringing the seeds you plant on your farms
From a land so far away, of a tree so tall and high
That the birds of the earth shall rest and nest

The flies shall perch from one plant to another
And pollinate one plant unto another
Different sizes and type they come
As they make your food, and shape your way of life

You continue to evolve, to live and grow
Each having a place of rest and peace of mind
An abode so simple and less stressful
But ours have no rest, no peace, and no home

Always flying, always watching, and always searching
With trees so short for us to rest and so scarce for cover
When anyone of you who see us wants to bring us down
For your meat or for the zoo where we don't belong

If only we can be envious or so jealous like you
We will not let you live for you can't hide from us
If only you are humble or know how to ask
We'll take less from you; in return we'll give you more

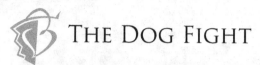

THE DOG FIGHT

The dogs are out feeding
The bones, the meat, and the flesh
Laid waste to the bones round the east gate
often around the south corridor

Bones on their neck in dangle
Blood dripping and dropping
Trickle trickle trickle in dungeon
Frail from pang of canine

Fighting constantly in battle of bait
A contest over nothing but humor
Fangs cutting deep amidst cruelty
Staged around the corner down south

Happening frequently elsewhere
downtown on the east side
Jumping on each other, heads lifted up
Legs scratching and eyes searching

Any opening; an opportunity for attack
wounds all over the body
where dark red fluid oozes
drip drip drip all over the floor

Jackal sees chunk of meat flying
Hector caught it in side view
Both let go of each other running
landing their teeth on the flesh

Dragging backwards with what is left
of their last energy and strength
hind legs fastened to the ground
as they pull and drag in fussy sound

Alerting each other of battle ahead
to win victory over the piece of meat
only for it to separate with each
being compensated with each part

For a job well done trying to kill each
Rewarded handsomely at the end
Before they kill each other in obedience
What a way to entertain and gamble

WHERE ARE YOU?

Where are you my good people?
Citizens scattered all over the globe
Across the depth and breadth of:
The savannah, the thick forest, and the desert
In the wilderness they search for it

Where are your life and future?
Hiding in a dream land
In the wild you traveled
Life and future hidden from all
Nature at work in a wonderland

Where are your secret keys of life?
Men at work against each other
Opposing nature so contradicted
Conflict binding humanity to its tiers
Piers of landing roughened by ages

Where are your fulfilling lives?
Each anchor hooked at edges
Each citizen left wide open
Their Will free and misused
By each abusing free will

Where is your free will?
Wicked spirit stepping and roaming
If only I can control you
My Lord will find me soon
Surely I am lost in the wilderness

Where are your wilderness?
Loud voice I heard calling out
Far and near I have gone to
in the deep and troubled water
Drowning and swimming head above water

Where are you hiding God?
In the depth and breadth I search
The savannah the thick forest the desert
Swallowed and covered in wilderness
Lonely place brothers and friends are lost

JUNGLE KINGDOM

Together they gathered in town hall
at the gate of the jungle kingdom
Argument upon argument made
decisions upon decisions in laws
children to attend school after school
without which hands are cuffed
freedom is lost and bodies in boxes

Knowledge resident in field places
dry land partitioned by four walls
life outside the walls excluded learning
each child nudged and pushed
learned or not what significance is it
managing the funding more important than learning
Pushing them and moving them one level to next

Test and pass them through the entity
help them if passed not through to the next
else funding ceases and our job is taken
So, push them along the way up as masters desired
At what expense our children sacrificed
shame on you, all you masters
children without future kingdom fails

REWARDING RELATIONSHIP AND GENUINE LOVE DIVINE

She seeks out every open field
Through cracks, crevices, and holes
Picking and peeping Tom through life
Coming and maneuvering from valley side
Searching and marching through the swamp
Hopping down the creek in confidence
Full of joy that the treasure has been found

Why too much faith in materialism made seen
Thinking like most men about green-fruited tree
The knowledge about life and death abound
And yet we are still lagging behind the truth
We don't know everything—anything
Someone does know everything—anything
Any and every knowledge about life and death

Because He lived and overcame them
One can live and overcome them too
You that trust Him but not trust him,
Man with mortal soul limited like you
Scheming and gaming to His heart by yourself
Leaving integrity based honesty behind
When that's not what you need in truth to win

Forgetting how vulnerable and exposed you're
Your heart and soul wide open in the green
Thoughts, words, and every calculated movement
Laid bare before Him through Him in wilderness
For that reason you had failed to capture his heart
The trophy desired and longed for lost to another
Your behavior and attitude manifesting itself now

Could you have been true to yourself and him
He would have learnt to trust you for you
Taking you for who you are, Samantha
Even if you are not the one to clench his heart
You are and will be who you are yourself always
A friendship forged at last, bond too strong to break
Rewarding relationship and genuine love divine

SPEAK THE TRUTH

When you stand before death, speak the truth
You traveler, speak the truth before man and woman
In difficulty speak the truth; in trial before the judge
Let your lips speak the truth before God who's the truth

As they gathered by the town hall he spoke the truth
Before the council he spoke the truth and we all heard him
In truth, those that lied against him were condemned
Even his accusers spoke his truth and we heard them

He walked out of the gate of the town we saw him
Free with his people carrying him on their shoulders
They rejoiced as he was set free; his truth saved him
We watched as he was persecuted and prosecuted

Why have we done nothing, what have we not done?
Stand up for what we believe in; our legacy to protect
To see innocent persons suffer; do nothing in their defense
To damage and cause permanent harm to our shared dream

It stinks like feces, excreta of a wild cat in the jungle
In its darkness the color of evil and the smell of demons
Encroaching into our lives are usurpers of our liberty
Squanderer of our freedom, justice, and our legacy

Caste them out; you demons, you evil, and you traitors
You betrayed your people, your fathers, and forefathers
Oh compatriots rise and dress yourselves in God's armor
In your mighty power take your stand against devil's schemes

In defense of our values, our democracy, and our nation
Gird yourselves with the belt of truth and stand in firmness
Let your feet be strong to carry the breastplate of justice
Your shield is triumphantly faithful to the sword of your spirit

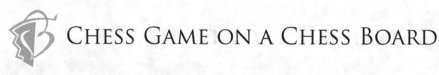

CHESS GAME ON A CHESS BOARD

It's a chess game on a chessboard
Tournament between an amateur and a pro
Each piece chasing one another for a kill
With skills consuming every thought on their fats
Planning and strategizing each play move

Each piece moving in specific runway
Like moves following same old rules
A path preset for each piece in rhymes
Both singing in harmonic lyrical beats
Moving forward backward left or right

The King makes no move in any direction
Protected by friendly allies; flanked by Nobles
Queen, Rooks, Bishops, Knights, and Pawns
Putting their life on the line protecting the King
The King follows to the left, right, front, and back

The Queen moves forth to hold the fort
Sensing danger to the King moves backward
Then moves to the left deflecting the assailant
As the enemy approaches she blocks to the right
With passion so dedicated to defending the King

The Rooks motion forward to embolden the front
Seeing dagger towards the King rushes backward
Thence hooves to the left defending him from assault
As the King's foes reaproach hopping to the right fortified
Without compassion so delicately guarding the King

The Bishops' hooks diagonally holding the barrier
Streaming power to the King's hoofs on vacant squares
Their moods predicated upon opposing colors on board
Each calculated unpredictable movement saves the King
Within reason cheerfully canceling foes of the King

The Knights' horses on alternate colors on board
Smelling danger to the King from a distance away
There they diagonally hop, kick, and cover the King
Jumping the hoops over opposing armies in defense
Castling their way in might and strength to blockade

The Pawn hosts them one step forward to a standstill
Storming two steps in the beginning and evading
To the left and to the right it maneuvers like Achilles
Jumping the hoops over opposing Armies in defense
Promoted to be Queen, Rook, Bishop, or Knight

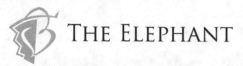

THE ELEPHANT

What an elephant mammal, you are created
What an elegant creature, you are
Very beautiful, very pretty
Like an angelic host, guarding its flock
What a gigantic creature, you've become

Do you know, there are ants
Do you notice them, Oh! Elephant
Do you think about them, when you step your foot
Yes, you can, you should; you do
What a sensitive creature, you are

So caring, so nurturing, so comforting
What a protective animal, you are
So domineering, so defeating
Even the king of the beast, is scared of you
The lions, the tigers, all and sundry

They dare not come near you
You come together, you stick together
Male and female, you form your family
With love and faithfulness, you spend your life
In compassion and kindness, you correct each other

With all your strength and might
you clear the path for you and your offspring
When you were born, though small
you were never stepped on
both parents were there, watching over you

Together, they fed, trained and groomed you
With mercy and forgiveness, they caressed you
They have laid courses for your future
Legacies for you to choose from
It is great to be an elephant

Why Are All of Us So Different from Our Parents

Why are all of us so different from our parents?
Families so genetically and independently deprived
Genes coming from the same father and mother
Engaging in a process of continuous reproductive variations
Oh! Epistasis!! Epistasis!! Epistasis!!! Epistasis!!!!
You cursed them all to be different
Where the dominant Alleles go to work
Where the recessive Alleles are laid to waste
John is as huge as Goliath
Joe is as short as Robert Wadlow
Peter is as tall as the pigmies
Lizza is a very beautiful blonde
Stacy is such an ugly brunette
Oh, chromosomes, where did you come from
From our father and from our mother
The handiwork of God, we are all one family

PART 2

HUMANISM AND SECULARISM

Mankind is constantly in conflict with its environment;
a product of their own milieu

A Little Boy Young and Restless

A little boy young and restless
Fragile, weak, and tender loving
Tending to the flocks in the field

A good Shepard is an asset for the farmer
Herdsmen are made but shepherds are born
You are a handmaid of a Master craftsman

Made you talented shepherd beyond reproach
With bare hands you can rip wide apart
The jaws and the head of a lion separated

The plants and animals listen in obedience
But your master sees just a little boy
Frail, not strong, and not fit for war

The nation is under attack
Surrounded by the enemies
East, West, North, and South

They trembled before the giant warriors
All armies rotten before their hands
Weapons amassed beyond defeat

Though you surrender you will not live
If you fight you will not live
What can anyone do oh God help

Here I come to fight you midgets
You worms matching on our land
Trying to devour our greens and sands

With laughter echoing through the nations
Neighboring nations trembling at the sound
The missiles flying from his hands

The giant of the giant's staggered steps
The warrior of the warrior's head hitting the ground
In dismay a hole is made on the ground

Where his head lay in waste, body stilled
His spirit already left the body turned cold
The trumpet blasted puaaaah in retreat

Standing strong heads looking up
Is the little boy young and restless
Called to the war front by his Master

He disobeyed his master to stay home
But obeyed his Master to defend his people
In fearlessness he routed the foreign armies

Our nation is delivered from their hands
Our enemies scattered in seven directions
We are saved by the handmaid of the Lord

 # GIVE THEM LIFE

Give them hope give them life
You parents give them future
Knowledge of life and death give them
To read and to write teach them

Dig the foundation before you build them
When they are laid pour the concrete base
After your labor pour the concrete pillars
As you feed them lay the bricks

Teachers lay the bricks and build the walls
Install the doors and the windows
A building needs plastering and painting
Educate and correct errors not blame game

Government builds roads and bridges
sewers utilities amenities and environment
Supplies of the people by the people for the people
guided with good policy and leadership

Just leadership breeds new leadership renewal
Some leaders are born while some are made
All in perpetuity and continuity of purpose
Of which life is given and wealth is inherited

You that are born furnish the house
One that is made follows their footsteps
To fulfill the purpose of which you are born
The reason for which you are made

 PUBLIC ENEMY

We have so many buildings on the block
The red bricks shining miles away
Like a board game from the aerial view
It shows equality amongst mankind
Each with every resemblance in every way

Every apartment occupied; every house filled
Each family resembling one another
If not in economics it is in social status et cetera
Brought together by circumstances of life
Now tapped into for a political advantage

Both claiming ownership to its politics
All fighting over their entitlement to it
Championship resident with the left
The right fighting for a winning chance
Awhile they had abandoned the program

In limbo they were left to rot
Both sides of the aisles of politics
Equally wrecking the project differently
Depraved indifference to the plight of the people
Political correctness of cheap short-term goals

Short sightedness ignoring long-term goals
To uplift people beyond their sustenance
Placed in the path to economic growth
Developing social status strong and high
Revitalizing capitalism with every renewal

The field is uneven for all players
Each playing on different strata
An abode borne by the people
Undertaking too expensive to carry
Residents not accounted to nor involved

Environment unworthy of a human nest
Springing chicks splinting in every corner
Mingling and commingling with each other
Sharing experiences that is chicken-hearted
Negative influences about reality of life

Downward trend life unfulfilled
Supported by the three arms of government
The people and the statehood burdened to death
If only the liberty, justice, and the freedom lacks not
The political will to change the paradigm will abound

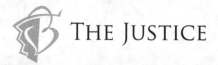

THE JUSTICE

Now comes Justice for all
In the matter of Just, integrity, Et. Al
Versus Truth, Righteousness, Et. Al
Before the honorable Judge
Both the plaintiff and the defendant are present

His name is the Counsel representing the Plaintiff
Her name is the Attorney representing the Defendant
Plaintiff filed a complaint against the Defendant
Defendant filed a counter complaint against the Plaintiff
Both seeking relief for violating each other's contract and rights

Claims of pains and sufferings in millions
Damages in millions, punitive damages in millions
Legal charges in thousands, interest charges in hundreds
All for nothing but ego soothing exercises
Chasing the worldly riches and glory

Over matters that could be amicably resolved
Conflict that's seeking harmonious resolution
By people whose harmonious coexistence
Depends largely on each other's talents and supports
Clustering our judicial dockets and laboring our judges

Plaintiffs and Defendants poking each other
With eyes wide open and mouth tied
Counsel and Attorney boxing in their suit
Each dancing, pacing, and moving back and forth
Both speaking through their solicitors and advocates

All performing in legal theater
Where everyone else is a spectator
Unless your name ends in Esquire
Then you can get a piece of the action
Justice available to the best boxer in the ring

Boxing skills more useful than the truth
Righteousness and integrity less attractive
The system not designed that way by default
The truth very difficult to prove without witnesses
Unless you are blessed with big and strong evidence

 # LOVE A DISTANCE

Quite a distance; N`chey I love you
In the morning; I love you, my darling
In the afternoon; I love you more
In the evening; I love you most
At night all calm and peaceful, I am consumed

In my thoughts I wonder in travel
In my imagination I wallow in lust
If only I can see you may be I will have you
In my bosom I shall lay you down
Beside me you shall be comforted

What awful thoughts in my mind
Foolish, dirty, and unclean such thoughts are
Unworthy of a child born of light
Lights shining from heaven above
You; I reject, rebuke, bind, and cast off my mind

Lest I reject, rebuke, bind, and cast off my life
the Holy Spirit, Jesus and God Almighty
Resident in His temple inside me
The working power of God deactivated
And be exposed to all forms of attacks

Evil in nature too weak and overpowered
Too frail my sovereignty compromised
If I sacrifice all line of defense around me
Thinking about you in a wrong way
In lieu of loving you in way of Christ

Your height figure eight complexioned
The beauty shapes and sizes of all
The work of a Master Creator God Himself
Craftsmanship beyond anyone or thing
Amazing handiwork of God in admiration

A way to honor worship and glorify Him
For making you a perfect creature
A beauty to behold in the eye of a lover
To be grateful to God for knowing you well
That one day we shall be one if He wills it

Then you will be ripe and ready for me
All thoughts shall become real not illusionary
Besides and around me no hollow found
Our minds bodies and souls becomes one
A match perfectly made in heaven and earth

Our life intertwined by the Master Potter's hand
Clay molded by the Holy Trinity in harmony
Homogeneously made in their image and likeness
Their Spirit breathed in us to start life anew
As one in two persons I call it Binity

THE MAN SHE LOVED SO DEARLY

He desires her for a divine purpose
Fulfilling the command of the Lord
In the beginning He created them man and woman

He left his house and went to her house
Cleaning, sweeping, dusting, and cooking
Making the bed, the room, and the house

She came home happy to see her love
With joy she went and kissed him warmly
In appreciation of the housework he's done

Surprising her was very loving and caring
Together they joined to complete the work
Started by the man she loved so dearly

His look amazingly surprised by her beauty
Complexioned and lightened by nature
Her size larger than his expectation

His mind cluttered with thoughts and ideas
In a wonder struggle of what he wants
The size or the spirit what is important

If only his wish and desire he will reject
Is not for him to decide but Him who commanded
The One and Only who put him to sleep and created her

YOU ARE THE ONE IN MY VISION; MAY BE THE ONE

Here I am at my home baby-sitting
Bouncing baby boy standing and stepping
Running towards the entrance door
Quickly I rushed grabbing prince charming

As I raised him up above my head
Like I was going to let go in the air
But presenting him before his creator
Behold there was a shadow, elegant and tall

Behind is a beautiful woman standing
Watching us playing but for how long
Smiling and chuckling in admiration
As a queen watches over her prince

Humbled by her poise and pose
With my right palm cupped around her cheek
Her left palm cupped around back of my palm
Our eyes meeting each other's gaze says it all

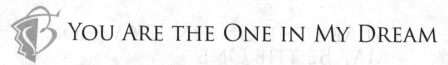

YOU ARE THE ONE IN MY DREAM

It was a dry winter day
Off to work I went, my bed properly made
In a house I live with everywhere quiet
The cream door opened my left hand swinging
On my bed lay a beautiful woman tucked in sleep

In rage, what are you doing here? I asked
How did you get in; all in one question?
Soft-spoken gently answered Jenny
I am in my home what do you mean
Then, I saw the face; it's the woman I desired

Jumping up in my sleep; it was only a dream
Here I am laying in my bed; the woman not around
How much I wished she was home; it was her home
In Morning Prayer I beseeched you Lord; Jesus Christ
That you bring me my Eve oh creator; God Almighty

THE TOWN WHERE YOU WERE BORN

Jenny my darling sister in Jesus Christ
Now that I've earned your privilege and honor
your trust and confidence in Jesus Christ
To the generosity of your heart and kindness
allowing me into your world and friendship
In my thanksgiving to you this morning
wondering what part of country you are from
The state you were born and your father's town
How tall you are and what are your first names
My intrusion hopefully excused by your reasoning
If you will be kind to quench my curiosity
it will be an honor to me knowing well
who my friend is her origin like Jesus of Nazareth
Our friendship to grow in bonding with His will

SOUTH BALTIMORE I LOVE YOU

This Project used to be our home in our town,
The pride of our community in our city,
When we used to matter to this city and state.
A nation offering reparation, appeasing its lows,
Building homes, families, and communities for its own.
A town within a town, a village within a village, a city within a city.

We used to feel great walking down the street and up the hill,
Safe as we visit one another in endless walks to and fro.
From one house to another we troop down to the harbor.
On the veterans bridge we stand fishing, dropping our strings.
We can hear each other's throw as the strings unwind,
Looking forward to who will make the first catch and biggest catch.

"Yeah," we shout out, "I got something," laughing and rejoicing.
As the cool breeze blows through our clothes into our bodies.
With excitement we watch as the drawbridge opens,
A ship passing into the harbor blowing its loud horn,
Announcing to every one of us that we have an august visitor.
We watch those that come through the high sea in front.

Containers lined up sitting on top of the carriers,
Arriving in different shades of blue, green, red, yellow,
Bringing bustling life to our family, community, city, and state.
Many of us laying on the grass overlooking the pier
Where our parents park their boat, making them feel important.
Part of our community, city, state, and nation's wealth and dreams.

Resting from a hard day's work at Baltimore gas and electric,
Close to Baltimore Sun, Bethlehem Steel, and Sparrow Point.
Where are Lord Baltimore, Thomas Sparrow, Fredrick Wood,
Pennsylvania Steel Co., Bethlehem Iron Co. of today?
Turner Station, Watersedge, Edgemere, Fort Howard of tomorrow?
Highlandtown, Edmondson Village, Brooklyn, your towns are gone.

I tell you my children, life was good, it was wonderful.
I tell you this to apologize that our generation let you down.
We squandered the legacy we inherited and passed nothing to you.
We have left you hopeless, helpless, and no future to look forward to,
But you are very resilient, stronger than we were, and have more chances.
I want you to use your head, innovate, invent, fight, and never give up.

 BALTIMORE

It was one spring morning at the south side,
Looking towards the east of the town in the city.
It was a beautiful scene to see the reflections
As sunlight refracts the magnificent city images,
The edifices and every structure shining through.

Behold, my eyes had seen the glamour and the glory.
Yellow rays brightened in moments of progressions,
Moving towards the center of the Earth to the west,
Setting with even better lighting than some mornings.
Really the Earth is moving towards south or northeast.

Sun starring in a static mode forever as the Earth rotates.
Depending on which side of the Earth you are standing,
What side the sun rises and sets, the Earth is visible,
The rays of its energy beams and radiates down on Earth,
Giving powers and life to its inhabitants and plants.

The greener the plants, the merrier the resources are.
A pleasing aroma rises and spreads down our street.
Like a dog, I followed the scent up and down and around.
There are flowers on every street, court, and every yard.
Different blooms and colors springing from green plants.

Elongated yellow tubular and some plain purple flowers.
I found violet, red, blue, green, and pink flowers alike.
Those found to be lavender, maroon, orange, or brown are few.
Colorful flowery arrangements dotted many green grasses
and lawns, curbs, and the flower beds of the development.

Each oozing out different aromas rarely differentiated afar,
close to your nostrils with hands gently pulling it close.
With every mindfulness of its delicacies and fragility,
You find the uniqueness of each pleasing pleasurable smell.
Oh gracious gift of God, your hands made these gardens.

A semblance of Eden in which you had planted men You created
Before they lost the privilege of being true image and likeness of Him.
We've lost that again though we now have Christ, believe in God.
My towns have changed it, transformed so fast and furious.
This is not the city I was born, where I walked miles in pleasure,

Sensitizing every sense: touched, smelled, saw, heard, tasted.
The gift of nature and ingenuity of my fellow man that planned.
Off to college I went, moving far away, wild wild west for pasture.
Greener and rich for feeding and grazing my flock, a Shepherd I am,
To fulfill the will of my father who commanded me as my Father did.

To procreate, to fill the earth, to conquer, and to subdue it.
In His glory, praise, and worship His intelligence abounds.
His honor, my honor, to obey the command of which I was given.
With all my strength, power, and might of my youthful life,
I shall labor, harvest, and reap what I sowed my dream to gain.

Here I return at my old age in retirement to rest in my hometown,
And the town has shifted and moved; my city could not be found.
Am lost, missed road, no road, bad road, the house is gone, unfounded.
The bricks are red, windows, plywood boarded, roads, blocked in holes.
Red and white cones, large cones, and yellow tapes dotted the land,

And the sidewalks, the curbs, the lawns, and the flower beds on yards.
My district is gone, my representation is extinct, I'll vote next district.
The faces I grew up with are gone, I see new faces of strangers everywhere
In between closed blocks and homes, grounds where we use to play,
The street where I walked for miles, east, west, and around with pride.

The businesses are closed, shops moved, churches full of homeless.
What have they done to my people, my town, my village, and my city?
Where are the developers, the planners, the policiers, and the leaders?
I fell down on my knees, my hands covering my face in shame and guilt,
And I wept, wailed, cried, and moaned in pains to see my town deserted.

The beauty, the glamour, the peacefulness, and the love evaporated.
We're the developers, the planners, the policiers, and the leaders.
Let's tear them down: the boards, the bricks, the roads, and the bridges.
Bring our people back to town to rebuild our home and our city.
We will rebuild our community, our village, our city, better than before.

All pavement, bricks, curbs, roads, bridges, businesses, and shops,
The memories, images, and sceneries that are buried in our fatty heads,
Waiting to guide us in replanning and reclaiming our enclaves and place.
The history will be made again to show the world how great we are.
Together with each other, the governed and the governors we will win.

History will be made again over and over until we rebuild for our children
A new community, new village, new town, new city, and new hope.
We owe them greater legacy than we inherited, a promised land we'll give
To our children, children's children, their life, future, our life, our future.
Dreamers that come to life in everything, with liberty and justice for all.

WHAT A BLESSING YOU ARE BORN TO US

My son, what a blessing you are born to us.
What a beautiful world greater than any other world.
Beware of their wickedness, those who live in it.
Embrace their caring and loveliness amidst of them.

My daughter, what a blessing you are born to us.
What a beautiful universe within a universe.
Be careful, treacherousness is prevalent among them.
Welcome those alive in truth and spirit, those not also.

They will stone both of you to death—not by rock.
You'll be stoned with silence, with words, and with actions.
Gradually your body will be dismembered in parts,
With each blow thrown at you not physical and biological.

They talk about freedom, liberty, and justice for both of you.
Majority live freedom, liberty, and justice for all mankind.
Be mindful of freedomless, libertyless, and injustice amidst.
Such stones are worst: more dismembering and destructive.

The reason many mistrust and resentment is everlasting,
Keeping people apart from each other separated by a thick wall.
Please do not be like them; the enemies of the State and do not fear.
Be not like those who clamor for civil rights, but only on their lips.

Those that perjure, bear false witness, and falsely accuse,
Those who prosecute, misconduct, and execute them,
They will make mistakes as human but cover it up.
They will convict you falsely and won't exonerate you.

False convictions will never stop; it is a career maker.
Some are just so stubborn, arrogant, and full of pride.
Those kinds of people will not come near your way of life.
I'm your mother warning you, and you will overcome them.

Behold your God, the Lord your savior, who created you.
He loves you more than anyone could ever be and He is powerful.
Be strong, persevere, and hand over all things to Him.
He is the king over all; His decree has set you free.

 # IT IS TIME TO LET GO

You that was enslaved have been set free long ago.
Though post-traumatically stressful, set yourself free.
It is time to let go of your past pains and sufferings,
And create opportunity for joy and future blessings.

Your father and forefathers slaved to their masters.
You're bound by their royalty the ties forged by history,
The hugging of the strings and the mind of slavery,
Without which you have no life, no future, no eternity.

Why still cling to the ties and strings that hold you back?
A life full of anger, grudges, malice, and bitterness
Towards those that set you free and slaved you not.
False sense of pride, unrepentance that cause you death.

The heart that is filthy and resentful is yours not theirs.
Their mind is free, for they feel neither sorrow nor remorse,
Because they owned no slaves, ever, nor lived with one, ever.
Their fathers and forefathers have all gone to their master

To reckon with Him who is the Master of the masters,
Grand Master who sent Master servant to save us all,
That we all may be cleaned of uncleanness and be set free.
Why then you're still bitter against those who slaved you not?

CHICKENS SPRINGING UP AS THEY HATCH

This is really how the world works, what family is?
In the shell it feels so warm and comfortable,
Mother sitting over the eggs brooding you warmth,
Being there in wait with hunger, thirst, 'til your birth.

With its beak it pecks the egg to open if not hatched,
In desperate desire and expectation of its children.
Chickens springing up as they hatch to mother's joy,
kwo-kwoing in tears of joy as the babies are born.

Before you know it they are grown to adolescents,
Teenagers passing through biological changes.
In chicken years they are grown in mother's light,
That pecks them to go until they leave their nest

In search of their own family, fending for themselves.
If only they grow together as a family a little longer,
Preparing for their separation working both attitudes,
Their life easier in comforting succor and fulfillment.

A Man Who Knows About a Thing

A man who does not know about a thing,
and does not know that he does not know, is a fool.
Don't just stay afar but run away from such a man.

A man who does not know about a thing,
and knows that he does not know, is like a child.
Don't just teach but show and lead him all the way.

A man who knows a great deal about a thing,
and does not know that he knows, is handicapped.
Don't steal his knowledge, guide him to it.

A man who knows about a thing,
and knows that he knows in sharing, is a wise man.
Listen to him; if he doesn't show off, follow him.

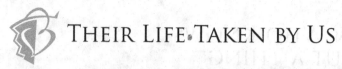

THEIR LIFE·TAKEN BY US

They came home from tiring national service
And found Jody sitting in the home they built
Hot meals served by their wives to Jody playing with their kids
Kicked out in the street passersby trod on the homeless dudes
With no understanding of how much they are suffering
Their sacrifices to keep us safe and protect our liberty
Not knowing who to go to and how to turn life anew
They give up hope and desire to live their life taken by us

It's a pity that to protect our freedom they lost their dream
The value for life we cherish and share they fought for
Defending us by defending the world from all kinds of rape
Monsters who abuse their own people and abuse the world
Their families sacrificed while their children suffer big losses
Their father or mother not being part of their life or growth
As strangers attend to their school meetings and every game
They give up hope and desire to live their life taken by us

They can bear it no more as they batter their spouse and kids
Swiftly they move their eyes three hundred and sixty degrees fearlessly
Fatigued by the scares of war without community integration
At the sound of a plane, the dropping of dumpster by dump-truck
They dodge under bed, under cover with flashes, gears in reach
If the door opens unannounced, they jump up reacting as in war
Memories of war relived many times, when there's no help
They give up hope and desire to live their life taken by us

Yet some people take their lives and their sacrifices for granted
Some do engage in crimes, killing, assaulting, and bullying
Like we bully those who suffer and die that we may live
Those we kill in series, in layers of words and actions
Looking down on others, even our own top commanders
The nobles, the gentlemen, and the ladies who love us most
In whose bloods, pains, and sufferings our justice thrives
They give up hope and desire to live their life taken by us

 WHO I AM AND WHAT I WANT IN LIFE I DON'T KNOW

Who I am and what I want in life I don't know
I do know that I do not want to be rich
Owning my business, being employer I want not
To invent, to innovate, to create, and to make isn't for me
However, to work, to help, to eat, to rest my head for sure
Jobless will sleep, wake, eat, sleep, wake, and eat every day

Many more sleep, wake, eat, play, and continue in cycle
If I can do so at another's expense, it is even the best
Why bother to work, invent, innovate, create, and make
Life is good, everything I want; I can get without work or study
To live deep on others, just to be clothed, and sheltered
Dwelling in melancholy, self-pity, and nonchalant to me

Lazy lizard on the fence preying on lame duck's resources
Pacified by mouth sucker made from saw dust
Providing no enrichment to the bodies though very tasty
Robbing their body of needed growth and development
Opportunity to mature and be strong like others
To compete with others providing for their needs

Ways to encourage and courage to realize their dreams
To be fulfilled, live to self-actualization of sense of purpose
To work, to help, to eat, to rest their head for sure
To sleep, wake, eat, sleep, wake, and eat every day
Many more sleep, wake, eat, play, and continue in cycle
To invent, to innovate, to create, and to make is for all

They have the talents, the gifts, and the skills to do so
And for those who do not, to follow those who do
Those who follow to work, to eat, and to rest for sure
Those being followed to lead, to dream, and to reign
Please let's think, let's dream, let's hope, and let's live again
Like our fathers, our forefathers for all is man made

My Last Evening with My Wife

She came to me in calm and compelling voice
Asking if there was anything I needed from the store
If I could taste the fruit smoothie she just compounded
In a very unusual friendly and respectful manner
Without her usual temper and angry outburst

I thought this is an unusual change of heart or attitude
Later she asked me if I could give her a ride somewhere
I remembered that is her way of being sweet before asking
I should've known there is something following her niceties
Her usual way of getting what she couldn't have got right away

If only she could be that caring always, great it will be
But full of attitude, impulses, and negative emotions
Yet I followed and took her to the store and to another
To the dry cleaners by Woodlawn six years last visited
the Goodwill store where she picked black pants and shirt

At home we arrived and I had to cook, clean and serve
Her, quiet as one preparing to mourn her spouse or loved one
I, playing the role of servant, which I am and always have been
That peace may reign in our home and love will overcome
Am expiring out of patience, my tolerance, and self-control

If you heard me please help, come to my aid else I die
Come quickly before melancholy consumes my life
Major depression is setting in please come, I can't breathe
She put me inside a closet with the door closed; a' claustrophobic
I feel like killing myself o' someone;—it-is—t-o-o-o-o mu—ch

SUCH NOBLE PROFESSION IN WHICH YOU ARE CALLED

It seem like yesterday, when she was in high school
Elizabeth and I thought, she will drop out of school
Like many of her peers and classmates running those joints
Surprisingly she did not; she went to our community college
We thought she was done after all her friends ended there
Her educational goal continued to our amazement and joy

She didn't want to be a stripper; has no looks to hustle
A sickle cell sicklier than all; my premature 6th child
Where will her energy come from, even if she wanted to be
Like many of her peers and classmates in our neighborhoods
She saw their lives, she heard their stories, and she hated it all
She left town for graduate studies; she wanted to save her pals

No one knew, she was on a mission; to save the world
Clarita came home different, deep in thought, and full of passion
Her mouth runs like water hose in talks and speeches to all ears
Everyone coming in and out of the house like a revolving door
All visitors confessing their sins, pains, sufferings, and frustrations
Out of pride, I volunteered to be her clerk, and support my child

Her mission and passion have gripped me like fever; am shivering
Together we will change our neighborhoods, town, and our city
Their children shall recover, be healed and free of their challenges
The feeling is great and the people are grateful a savior has come
To free them from their sins, pains, sufferings, and frustrations
It's like a life in hell while still alive on earth the end at no sight

Oh! Things have changed, my daughter is confessing to her father
Her pains, sufferings, and her frustrations about her profession
Although she is a licensed professional at United Care Poor Limited
Her work is regulated, mostly by those who are not licensed
Bureaucrats working their way through the structures of governance
It is not about the fruit of your labor but what the papers said

Your words and actions has no value; they have no time for that
The people don't count when the regulators err or after you
Her work is dead, her passion, and mission rescinds in her vision
The powers that is, the authorities of ages are pouncing on her
The light is snatched and has been hidden deep under the bushel
Her peers, classmates, neighborhoods, town and our city is dying

Who shall rise above pettiness and nothingness to save them all
Those whose work is for the sake of work that they may be paid
Those who work with passion, dedication, and care to save them all
To change the neighborhoods, town, city, and the world left behind
In the journey to the end and the purpose of which are unknown
Coded and decoded by those with the power to code and decode

Executed by those whose friends and likes are lofty and mighty
That search for pastures wherever is green by which means available
My poor little girl what a waste of talent and resources into your vision
So it seems but there is life and therefore hope should be great
Remember your speeches before your mission to save the world
Meditate on reasons and principles on which you centered your life

Through the knowledge and belief that your tutors and mentors gave
You were able to believe in yourself and purchase their sense of purpose
To be different from your peers and classmates but not indifferent
As their sins, pains, sufferings, stress, and frustrations overwhelms
Never forget who you are the purpose you are who God said you are
Think not and worry not of how to be like those allowed to be

To care not, give not and work only for all you can get from them
For that will be an end to you, for you to be who God wants you to be
An end to your mentors, who God used to make you who you are
And will be the end to such noble profession in which you are called
The people will get less and less quality in the service they receive
That definitely is not what you believe in or wish to be part thereof

THE USURPER IS COMING

There were dreams, visions, and pragmatisms
There were labors, rules, successes, and achievements
And the envy, the jealousy, and the haters in disguise

There were dreams; I saw them when they came in
In their colors, they blended in; walking into my life
Before they came I heard a dream and then, I waited

Then my assistant came to me saying I had a dream
The powers and principalities have conspired against you
They will take everything you have worked for in your life

Nothing will be spared, you will beg but they won't listen
We have to pray, we have to fast, for God to save your work
I laughed, with curiosity Ms. Little queried for laughing matter

Sit down please I said, I had the dreams several months ago
We have always prayed to frustrate the plans of the wicked
They will retreat, strategize, and come back in assault

The greatest power and principality belongs to God Almighty
He sees our heart, soul, and labor; He is just and righteous
Nothing placed in His hands can be taken by any person or spirit

He started this, He always finish what He started; I consoled
Do not worry my dear; we will be here when they come
We will go wherever they take us; where the Lord allows it

If they take it, look around there is something bigger waiting
No one came, we waited in expectation, and then they came
We're there as they parade the scene and took charge; everything

In chains they tied them, and in drags they carried everything
With our eyes we watched, quietly we left them in their control
Every one of them and everything we left in the hands of God

I went home with peace in my heart and slept like I never did
Answering every call and appearing in every court am dragged to
Waiting; expecting full of hope and faith, for my dreams to alive

At times I cried, at times I moaned, and at times I feared
Wondering what the future holds; the next chapter entails
Waiting to venture again into the dreamland; into the future

MAKING A CAREER IN THAT FIELD

That was a marvelous speech Mr. President
She thought out loud listening to him
Then she started pondering in day dream
Dreaming of becoming a helper; a civil servant

I wondered myself what she was looking at
Stop! Come back later; I'm trying to think
Oh, she was thinking about what he said
That's my gal; my sweet guardian angel

She will become a nurse or social worker
Caring for the sick, the poor or the elderly
With that much people getting some help
More hands will be needed to serve them

No! You got it all wrong, you got it all wrong
I am thinking about me; what's there for me
I am going back to school to get my masters
To get certified and be licensed professional

Don't you see that, can't you see the future?
That means more money than ever before
More job security and more stability for me
Making a career in that field; the helping career

I see me in a decade, rising a shining star
Rotating from one department to another
One position after another riding on a speed rail
with my pocket book full of green papers

You are really dreaming indeed my darling
You know I did not raise you like that
Thinking of yourself alone, without those families
In this crisis, financial meltdown, and sufferers

I thought you are undertaking another studies
Because you believe in its disciplines and values
In a principle centered ethics that helps others
And drives your passion; firing up your strength

If you do that you will not be happy
Success will elude you, and you'll find it unfulfilling
You may be wealthy but very miserable in life
Trust me I know because I have been there

THE BLAME GAME

Did you hear what I am hearing?
It sounds like everything around
When you turn to your television
Try to listen to the radio and rejoice
And what do you see on the street
Every nook and corner; in coffee shops
Someone is always blaming another
Accusations and counter accusations
Starting from the head down to the toes
What has that done and what has it changed
It's just a blame game and everyone onboard
Ineffective and inefficient way of life
To gossip, to judge, to condemn, and to punish

Oh! Solutions are always in the game
Problems are solved through blaming
Ownership and responsibility taken by players
Encouragement and empowerment are the rules
That governs, leads, manages, and administers them
Blame game helps to clearly set the goals
It clearly sets the standards for the players
It helps them to do what they are supposed to do
Those clearly qualified and credentialed by blaming
Blame clearly motivates people and teams
To clearly collaborate to form a winning team
Blame game is how to achieve desired outcome
One achieves efficiency and effectiveness by blaming others

COME TO OUR AID OH HOLLYWOOD

When we were growing up
we always watched fashion shows
Our eyes fixed at the TV to see
the Hollywood actors and actresses
Stars shining from Beverly Hills
to the Valleys of the Silicon

From the shorelines of Florida
to the wastelands of Texas
Every eye in the skylines of New York
to the ends of the earth watches
Just to get a glimpse of how to look
We did not copy their fashions only

We lived like them in every way we could
We observed their nutrition and cooking
watching our weight to see our BMI
That we may look like them, as copycats
Though we focused on our looks and sizes
We really prevented many sicknesses

Our health and economy were better
Our country was richer and stronger
Oh Hollywood, your Beverly Hills brags
You told us to worry not about our BMI
To be proud however we look, loving us
Our self-esteem not affected by our sizes

We have lost it in giant and extra sizes
Squandering our health and good riches
The death of sons and daughters abounds
These debilitating illnesses bankrupting us
Our self-esteem destroyed at self and country
Come to our aid oh Hollywood save us all

 # LOVE YOURSELVES

Why are some people blinded in spots?
Seeing in prisms and short angles
Do they see anyone but themselves?
Can they see beyond their nose?
Can they smell other than themselves?
Can they feel other than themselves?
Can they hear other than themselves?
Can they taste anything than their spit?

Some people see in three Dimensions
Three hundred and sixty degrees; they see around them
They see others around their surroundings
They perceive beyond their universe and senses
They see your strengths not just your weaknesses
They meet you wherever you are; they reach out
To you they meet half way into your life journey
They hold your hands walking into your future

You complain that you aren't loved by dear one
Where are the ones you love including yourself?
Do you love anyone other than yourself?
Do you love your neighbor as you love yourself?
You complain that you receive nothing from others
Where're the ones you've giving to; except yourself?
You complain that no one does anything for you
What are the things you have done for others?

For you to be loved by others;
is for you to love others
For you to be loved by your neighbors;
is for you to love your neighbors first
For you to receive from others;
is for you to give to others
For one to do anything for you;
is for you to do something for others

Spooky Sparky

Spooky! Spooky!! Spooky!!!
What? What the F— you woke me up for?
Who! Who the F— you are talking to?
Ma! I'm trying to get some sleep here.
Why? You keep bothering me; every morning?
You keep bothering me.

How many times have I told you?
Told me what?
That your mouth'll get you out of my house
No, it won't! It's my house!! I pay the bills!!!
Don't you ever think; your drug money
gives you right to disrespect me

I am your mother spooky
you can only have one mother
I am telling you now spooky
Oh! My goodness; nigga is
trying to get me some sleep here
Every morning nigga can't sleep

Am tired of this shi— ma
am getting out of here
Yes! Get out negro
I've been trying to wake you up
Since six O' Clock I have been trying
But you play it down, dead-fool, full of ignorance

It's time to get ready for school
you won't listen; you ain't listening
Told you ain't going to school
nothing there for me; we all can't go
Just to make you happy; I went
That you may get off my back

Get it over with!
And then what?
Run the street like jaguars
Yo! Make me some money; real money
Will buy you a house ma
Move you out of this project

No! I am worried of you going to jail
Just like your father did
Why bring my father into this?
Don't like when people talk about my father
He is dead! Can he lay in peace? He-he-he
Sorry my only loving son; don't wanta lose you

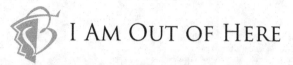 # I Am Out of Here

Alright ma; am out of here
I love you
I luv ya
Don't break my door; slamming it like a storm
Oh God help my son and watch over him
What can I do without my son?

Hey spooky! Was up yo!!
Was up nigga? Where are you going?
I am going to school; my name is James
I told you that
I don't like that word
'Tis demeaning to us; derogatory to our race

What did you just called me dog?
What! What do you mean?
The name deeeeeeee whatever
Oh! You mean demeaning and derogatory?
That is not a name; it is a word
Whatever yo, what does that mean?

You see; if you come to school
you will know the words
are you going to tell me or what?
You like big words anyway
I am serious; you can learn so much
Hey stop tripping dog, before I bang you

Alright! It means humiliating and disrespectful
to us and black race
What's wrong with you man
And stop calling me dog; I am human
Just left the house running from her mouth
Here you are sounding like her

Who? Your mom? I wish she is my mother
Nothing spoil man, just call me by my name
That's cool James, Saint James, Apostle James
Look, you still go to that Church
Which church are you talking about
Don't you know the one?

We use to go when we were kids
Yo! Why you don't come to church anymore
Don't have time for that no more
And who wants to know James?
You're not my father
He is dead, shot, never, never got to know him

So, don't talk to me about God
I understand, don't cry
You know I miss him too
You remember when
he use to drive us around
I am 17 years old James

Ain't got to go to school
Alright my brother
I don't mean to upset you
I am just looking out for my brother
I miss hanging out with you
Alright my brother, peace out yo!

 # MY FATHER; I AM CONFLICTED

Oh! James, why remind me of my father, my childhood?
I miss my father, oh! Father, I miss you.
When he used to buy me everything, I needed.
Never lacked from my father, Oh! Father why you.

He used to make us sing, we used to rap together.
Now can't sing with my father, never to sing with him.
He used to own the streets, used to ride with him.
Now streets are free for all, free for grabbing by any.

I miss my father, oh! Father, I miss you.
I wonder if my father would like what I am doing.
What was he doing? How did he make his papers?
Never saw him go to work, never broke, always full.

What did my father do, maybe a drug dealer?
Never knew him, too small to remember.
What he wanted me to be, I need to know.
I always hear my mother, Oh! Mother you hate him.

I don't want my son to be like you, James.
Yo! His name is James; you're going to kill my son.
My father always said, "read for me."
I miss my father, oh! Father, I miss you.

He always asked about my school, my homework.
I was six, never saw him read or write,
But always asked me to read my books; study,
You will be a doctor, a lawyer, A somebody.

Never be like your father, be A somebody?
Mother always says, who is my father?
What does that mean, be A somebody.
Was six, am seventeen, I am somebody.

But there is no future for me in school.
I have a felony conviction, been to jail.
Which school will admit me, if I make it?
Who will employ me, if I qualify?

Our system! Once stricken, forever stricken.
Forgiveness and rehabilitation, ends in jail.
Though we say, he has done his time,
He is never forgiven; his future is in the streets.

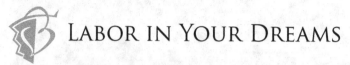

LABOR IN YOUR DREAMS

What exactly are we doing?
What are we buying with our tax dollars?
What is it that you are paying for?
My people, we should ask questions,
We should have expectations.

Where is the accountability?
Where are our values and integrity?
Who is looking out for our interest?
My people, we should stand upright,
We should reach out to those working for us.

Hey! You said you have visions.
You set a mission to fulfill them.
You came to us for a mandate,
And that we gave you.
We've never held back from you.

Why are you wasting what we gave you?
You throw them away; you trample them.
On frivolous things you spend them.
What about your visions, your dreams?
Where is the mission to your visions?

How much did you put in your mission?
Can the wasteful life wait 'til later?
When your visions and dreams come true,
That you may give to those who gave you,
Then you can reap from labor in your visions.

 # MY QUEEN

The prince of the jungle goes to school
To keep the queen from breaching the law.
The king absconding with a total stranger,
His throne abdicated for the queen's mother,
The queen struggling to reign over her subjects.

Prince of the jungle, where are you hiding?
It is time to go, before the queen is dethroned
For neglecting and abandoning her duty to us.
Failing in her duty to his soldiers at war
To train, to school, to educate, and to work.

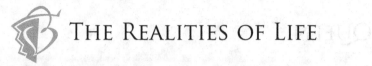

THE REALITIES OF LIFE

Off to school I went, to keep the queen safe.
Off to work I went, to keep the queen rich.
Off to the streets I went, to keep the queen poor.
Her honor free from dragging it through the mud
Because I chose not to do what is right and just.

At school I play, I curse; I fight, and am suspended.
I play with my peers, I play with my mates, and I play with my friends.
I curse at my peers, I curse at my teacher, and I curse at my enemies.
I fight with my peers, I fight with my teachers, and I fight with my foes.
I am suspended, am expelled, and I'm a dummy.

At work I play, am lazy, am unproductive, and I am fired.
I play with my peers, I play with my mates, and I play with my friends.
I loaf; loiter; and lounge about, I cover up my deeds.
I lie; deceive; cheat; stab; block; and frame my mates.
I'm stealing, defrauding, and abetting my peers and bosses.

At home I play, am lazy, a drunk, a criminal, and poor.
I play with my food, my peers, my video games, and my life.
I curse at my kids, my spouse, my parents, and everyone.
I fight with my kids, my spouse, my parents, and anyone.
I am illiterate, am jobless, am sick, am dying, and I'm poor.

In my hands are my life, my past, my present, and my future.
At school, if I play, curse, and fight, I will fail and be useless.
At work, if I play, loaf, lie, fraud, and cheat I will be fired.
At home, if I overplay, curse, fight, and hate I will be homeless.
In my life, I will be careful, work hard, persevere, and be fulfilled.

SPARKY SPARKY

Sparky Sparky is sent to school,
Where he went to learn to read,
Whence he'd learned to add and subtract.

Sparky Sparky ran from science to arts,
Where he went to learn to be great,
Hence he'd learned to act the art.

Sparky Sparky is afraid of science,
Where he won't succeed to be great,
Thence he'd scorned the act of reasoning.

Sparky Sparky changed his name,
Once he named himself as Spooky,
Then, he's in and out of his mind.

ALEX I LOVE BUT SMITH I HATE

Alex I love, but Smith I hate.
Wayne I hate as much as Smith.
Wayne and Smith are full of hatred.
Wayne is his father as Smith is my father.
Wayne is black and Smith is white.

Alex I love, because it is my name.
His name is Damonte, the love of my life.
What's wrong with that, we're all the same.
When Smith was dying, Damonte gave his kidney.
When Wayne was sick, my sister gave her blood.

Alex is my name, my heart is broken.
What color is his kidney, what color is her blood?
What colors are my cells, what colors are my genes?
What a hell is booked for those discriminators
That can't tell me why; they are underdeveloped.

Alex is alive, but Alex is hurting.
What's the use of life if I can't be with him?
My family's sworn to their grave that I will never be with him.
They took my life with them, when they banned him forever.
How can I be happy, without the people I love?

Damonte my love, what a hell your life is.
Your people hate you too, for loving Alex.
Alex, your beloved, can't pass the blockades.
Sisters in her face, everywhere she goes.
Brothers in pursuit, anytime she leaves.

We are in a new era, many centuries behind.
Living in our past, where racial pride thrived.
Blind to the present, norm to the future.
What era are they, which dwell in the past?
Help me my people, if you heard my cry.

BECAUSE I AM WHITE

Because of the color of my skin, because I am white.
Where is the future promised to me by my father?
The legacy left for us by our forefathers,
The dreams of our founders, our dreams and our life.

Because of the color of my skin, because I am white.
They told me my life has been made, an easy rosy one.
That my life will be easy, and a rosy jolly ride.
Maid and men servants will be at my beck, call, and wait.

Because of the color of my skin, because I am white.
That I am a prince and heir to the throne of my race.
Multitude of men ready to carter: for me, my needs, and my family.
Ready to work, to labor, and to serve, to the benefit of my race.

Because of the color of my skin, because I am white.
Where is that life and where is that promise?
Where is that future and where is that legacy?
Where is the servitude and where is the laborer?

Because of the color of my skin, because I am white.
Where is the dream and where is the opportunity?
I want to go to school but was cut off by a quota.
Even though my score is higher than others, I was cut off.

Because of the color of my skin, because I am white.
I applied to be employed but my application was rejected.
Even though I was the most qualified, the quota cut me off.
I couldn't get the job, just like the school I really needed.

Because of the color of my skin, because I am white.
I worked my blue color job and created my own business.
I pay my taxes, an endless circus and always increasing.
It is used to feed, pay for their education, and house the poor.

Because of the color of my skin, because I am white.
These people, these immigrants, who stole my dreams,
Who took my job, my education, and my money.
These people for whom I was discriminated against.

Because of the color of my skin, because I am white.
They can't work, don't work, don't want to work.
They have no home, can't buy, can't rent, and homeless.
Not their fault, not my fault, and I still pay for it.

Because of the color of my skin, because I am white.
I'm not a master, never owned a slave, and have no inheritance.
Born to false promises, helplessness, and no legacy.
In trying to fit in, I extend my hands to another race.

Because of the color of my skin, because I am white.
They left my hands hanging, reject me, and left me lonely.
They see my forefathers when they look at me.
They hate me so much when I try to be like them.

Because of the color of my skin, because I am white.
I can't marry one of them; I can't live with them due to hatred.
Why are the sins of our fathers, revenged against their children?
Our children, your children, our future, your future, our nation.

Because of the color of my skin, because I am white.
I can't take a walk on every street nor could they do the same.
I can't trust them just as they could not trust me.
I can't breathe, I can't stand the heat, and I am about to explode.

Because of the color of my skin, because I am white.
Those that energize this hatred and that keep us divided.
The paranoia of ignorance, fear of the unknown, and self-destruction.
Save my life, save my family, and save my children.

Because of the color of my skin, because I am white.
Please end this hatred, end this division, and end this wickedness.
Come and sit around my table or invite me to sit with you.
Let's hash out our common interests and values.

Because of the color of my skin, because I am white.
Let us reconcile our differences, with respect to each other's beliefs.
Let us work diligently through the pains of our past.
Let's stop pretending, deceiving each other, and be honest to ourselves.

Because of the color of my skin, because I am white.
It is time for reconciliation and a time for peace.
It is time for equality and a time for justice.
It is time for freedom and a time for liberty.

Because of the color of my skin, because I am white.
It is time to rebuild our nation and a time for unity.
It is time to dream again and a time for opportunity.
It is time to embrace each other and a time to love.

ARISE COMPATRIOTS YOU ALL ARYAN NATIONS

The changing world of the Aryan race,
Losing its splendor and Fraternal Order.
Where whites are the kings and queens,
Issuing all decrees and orders of liberty,
Dictating who lives and dies,
Deciding who wins or loses,
Driving who fails or succeeds,
Owning superiority over all other races.

Where are you oh Aryan compatriots?
You who fought to enthrone our race.
You who dethroned every other race.
Stop this madness of equality,
Being the same as those who once served us,
Those created by God to be our maids and servants,
Pieces of properties to help build our wealth,
And amuse and entertain our leisure and pleasure.

Give them not your children and marry them not.
Share not with them and deny them their rights.
Keep them in chains without using the steel.
Bring them down that ever climbed over you.
Step on anyone who stands in your way.
Our race will forever reign in brotherhood.
Those promoting equality are working against us,
Wiping out our race through intermarriage.

If you love yourself, stop that, now or never.
If you love the Aryan race, protect it from annihilation.
If you love your children, protect their legacy.
If you love your grandchildren, plan their future.
The Aryan race can't get in the school of their choice.
The Aryan race can't get the employment of their choice.
The Aryan race can't get with anything of their choice.
Arise compatriots, you all Aryan nations.

THE WASTELAND OF AMERICAS OF NATIVE DESCENTS

The wasteland of the Americas of Native descents.
The land of milk and honey in plains, hills, and valley sides.
The Earth ruled by the sun, moon, and the stars.
The creatures of the Earth in harmonious divine.

Overran and overtaken by the greed of intruders
That enslaved our bodies, minds, and souls.
Beaten, tortured, maimed, hurt, and suffered.
Defeated painful death prescribed over us.

No winner and no vanquish saved our dignity,
Bringing peace and harmony in coexistence
Of tribes and nations within one nation,
Our rights and sovereignty so intertwined.

Our Gods and alien gods appeased by our peace.
The wellness of our bodies, minds, and souls,
Availed to our citizens embracing our unity.
The blessings of the gods and goddesses abound.

The God of the gods and goddesses are alive
In every one of us that knows who He is,
Through our connections and life with all creations,
By seeking to reunite and transit into our spirits.

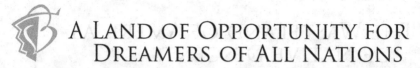

A LAND OF OPPORTUNITY FOR DREAMERS OF ALL NATIONS

Strangers, aliens, and foreign troops
Embarking on a journey to a foreign land.
Each hungry Jack, Javez, and Jackals,
Wondering, hiding, and stealing our crops,
Invading our farms, barns, and treasure rooms,
Passing through every crack and crevice,
Tunneling and burrowing through every ground,
Eating and squandering every spoil found,
While the land scrambles, running helter-skelter.

This land, their land, and our land,
Embalming the dead policy wronged.
Each patch work, hard work, and ancient rules
Pondering why the brains are sleeping it off.
Undaunted by uncounted immigrant masses,
Inducted by the generosity of their hearts,
Passes granted by every inbounding legalist,
Grooving, grooming, growing power and might,
Where the people and our people forgot who they were.

Driving them out and bringing them in.
Outbound ferries and inbound trailers.
Hauling and pulling of the tug-of-war
That shifts nowhere but to our growth and trade-offs.
Renewing our strength and weakening our bones
To the east, to the west, to the north and the south.
Their presence is as good as their menacing discomforts.
This land, our land, has become a united nations,
A land of opportunity for dreamers of all nations.

PART 3

RELIGIOSITY AND SPIRITUALISM

*The desires of the flesh are constantly in conflict
with the desires of the spirit.*

THE BONE OF MY BONE AND THE FLESH OF MY FLESH

Your spirit is troubled by my last verse,
Still hesitating to communicate involvement.
I am confusing or the confused message unclear.
Was told to tell the pastor first before you.
Thought you should know, first planned to ask,
But you were gone before I could turn around
And plan to ask the pastor and pastoral court
For assistance next month in seeking the Lord.
His confirmation as to the one of my rib.
The bone of my bone, and the flesh of my flesh I seek.

My Eve a handmaid of the Lord, a Potter's craft.
That request I could not make without you
Being in agreement in the spirit and ready
To accept the will of your Creator if He wills it,
As an obligation to which you have committed.
For it's written to be so in Numbers thirty in three.
Before I approach your family and Christ's body,
Reason for asking for your father's town,
I need to know in order to act on it, hope you do.
The bone of my bone and the flesh of my flesh I seek.

With great understanding and respect I ask
That you be open-minded, a place you stand
No matter how unusual church binding rules
Its effects to face to face time, place, and everything.
I just noticed you took me off as your social network friend.
Can you tell me my offence so that I can learn from it?
It's my understanding dating will be allowed while in prayers.
If confirmed marriage course and traditional can go on.
Physically you resemble my other half I've been searching for.
The bone of my bone and the flesh of my flesh I seek.

I see a female resemblance of myself in your looks.
Because I have given total control of my life and myself
To Jesus Christ and belief that God created Eve for Adam,
I have refused to pick a wife; I have been praying for a helper
For several years among all the ladies that were interested in me.
For years now there're few left still standing in my favor,
and of them one person is you; if it is God's will you'll be me.
I saw a vision and a dream which my brothers in Christ,
narrated as a prayer-answered; revelation in waiting.
The bone of my bone and the flesh of my flesh I seek.

God, having heard my prayers, once given approval.
Have a special relationship with God moving me only,
Acting according to His command or else I fail.
As much as I desire you, I hope He agrees you're the one.
I asked God to kick fake ones out and cut off the noise.
Even when I try to hold unto, He takes them away.
Though I have the gifts of the spirit, I am still a human.
I can see your heart, spirit, and soul up there giggling.
God had shown me to you but you're struggling with it.
The bone of my bone and the flesh of my flesh I seek.

You're not sure, wondering what you're sensing or feeling.
Prayer will clarify God's will, His purpose for both of us.
I know it's a lot which is why I thought you should know.
You deserve a heads up and time to process this innuendo.
A divine thinking to see if you are ready for matrimony.
Have enough time to ask yourself if you see yourself
Living with me, spending the rest of your life with me.
You are right, for a woman's feelings comes from emotions first.
You've to be involved with a man emotionally to feel something.
The bone of my bone and the flesh of my flesh I seek.

Men mostly develop feelings from what they see first.
You can also check and see if you find me attractive.
You can ask God for the Adam you're looking for.
If He says not that you find your Adam in me, it's alright.
If not you will accept me if God said I am the one.
In my second book I said that God does not violate any.
He does not infringe on anyone's personal sovereignty.
Church cannot make you marry someone you don't love,
Someone that you aren't meant or unwilling to love and marry.
The bone of my bone and the flesh of my flesh I seek.

It is your God but your call, your decision, and your life.
You will choose but who makes the decision: you or God.
That's why I needed to know if you're willing to obey,
To accept God's direction even if that's not your preference.
Mostly mankind doesn't, then we go through trials and tribulations.
Imagine the pastor coming to tell you after fasting and prayers,
The revelations shows I am your husband, without your input.
Of course you have a choice to reject it, but at what cost?
I'll wait until you process this revelation, able to say yes or no.
The bone of my bone and the flesh of my flesh I seek.

Yes it is a lot to think about, so much to consider now.
It is time to pray with concentration, focus and be specific.
The Lord God will guide you if you beseech Him in truth.
If it is the will of God, He will speak to you momentarily.
Pay attention to your dreams and voice of God in quiet times.
Reach out to me, your elders, and the pastors if you need to.
When I said yes or no, I mean surrendering to God completely.
Willingness to accept me if He says yes and brother if no.
Christian maturity that gives God absolute control of one's life.
The bone of my bone and the flesh of my flesh I seek.

I am hoping to hear the Lord say this is the woman with faith,
Made from your rib; come, see, and ask her to marry you.
After that go and see her family, that is our Lord's command.
Then I will be happy for He has made one of my own kinds
My companion, my other half, my equal, my co-creator with God.
We shall leave our family and join to become one in Christ.
Two, but one in perfect unity with God divinely born again.
Though we were two, will no longer be two, but become one.
New creation homogeneously and harmoniously transformed.
The bone of my bone and the flesh of my flesh I seek.

MY PEOPLE, WHY ARE WE STILL SO DIVIDED

My people, why are we still so divided?
We are one nation indivisible under God.
In God we stand; do we still trust?
Have we forgotten, not long ago?
A man had a dream, about our children.

They will sit together around a table.
They will eat, and they will drink.
Together, they'll hold each other's hands.
They'll sing and pray for His provisions.
They'll dream in abundance of His reaches.

He that's on top, squirt, stretch your hands down.
Hold your compatriots, stand, and lift them up.
Please give them a seat on your table.
Expand your platform that they may stand.
When they stand with you, help them to stand firmly.

Because they will in return hold your hands,
That you may stand on their shoulders,
Reaching out a new height above you.
They will hand you the tools and the materials
To build a new platform above all heights

On that new platform you shall climb unto,
You will reach new heights and new places,
Because you held each other's hands.
Because you pulled them up, you are blessed.
Your wealth has been increased abundantly.

Those that sat in the same platform alone,
Held no hand or hands of those like them alone.
They held fewer hands than they could have.
They built weaker or no platform to grow.
They held themselves down, holding others down.

Those that pulled others up, pulled themselves up.
They are foresighted, full of knowledge and wisdom.
They understood that diversity is strength for new heights.
They built a massive army around their defense.
Their life and investments are forever protected.

A FRIEND IS THE ONE LIKE YOU

Friends are the greatest assets anyone can have.
If you don't have any, please find some around you.
But who is a friend; what does it mean to you?
A friend is the one that always loves you
In your sickness and in your strong health.
In your poverty and in your riches, they stand by you.
When you are hot, they blow you like an oceanic breeze.
When you are cold, they blow you like a heat blower.
In challenges, they bring blissful joy to your heart.
When you are hungry, they bring food to your table.
When you are thirsty, they pour water on your tongue.
When you are lonely, they make comforting company.
When you are blessed, they celebrate with you.

A friend will not stab you, not even in your back.
A friend will not back-slide you, will not hold you back.
A friend will not kick you out or push you off the cliff.
A friend will not side-kick or put stud for you to fall.
A friend will not gloat or rejoice at your downfall.
A friend will not gossip about you or your family.
A friend will not bear grudge against you.
A friend will not keep record of your wrongs.
A friend will not be rude, selfish or envy you.
A friend protects you and your family's interests.
A friend is like a taste of honey on your tongue.
A friend trusts and rejoices with the truth.
A friend is the one like you in equal respect.

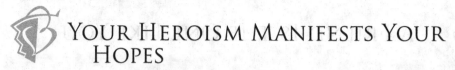

YOUR HEROISM MANIFESTS YOUR HOPES

What a faithful servant of the Lord you are.
With steadfastness, you discharge your duties.
Noble man standing elect before his electors.
Sentry before His Highness, waiting for His command
To give his life in service to his compatriots.
With a sense of duty he carries His command.

My Dear John, if not your faith what else?
Your courage subdues your fears and wimpiness.
Your heroism manifests your hopes and Godly trust.
How could you have survived without Him?
Your beliefs and your actions in one accord with Him.
That affected your faith! Without hope, it would've no effect

YOU WORRY TOO MUCH MY DARLING HUSBAND

You worry too much my darling husband.
The economic recession and depression will end,
And you will not be affected due to your faith.
Look inside you; what do you see Honey Burnie?
The Rock of Ages sitting inside your foundation,
Your body, mind, and soul sacrificed to Him.

There is no need for you to be disappointed.
My rock, please be strong, and be patient.
It is already well with us and rejoice with me.
The hand of the Lord is upon us and upon them.
His blessings are pouring down on us, you see!
His curses are upon them that caused you pain.

Remember! He is God of justice; vengeance is His.
Oh sweetheart, keep watch with me and see His actions.
Observe the punishment of the wicked around us.
Be patient and hopeful; after perseverance are His blessings.
Have faith knowing that we asked in the name of Jesus.
Believe that we have conquered, and victory is ours.

I LOVE YOU WITH ALL MY LIFE

Oh my beloved, forgive my doubts and my fears.
Wife of Godly nature who could reject,
Heavenly sent to me for a purposeful life.
He that finds her, waste not your life elsewhere.

When you are awakened at midnight, she's awake.
Before you think of evil, she whispers good words.
Before you ponder on worldliness, she speaks heavenliness.
Her voice is always a classic melody in your ears.

Like frankincense her breath tickles your body.
In each other's arms, you tangle in celebrations.
Rejoice! You who found love in your Eve.
The gift of love you both share is divine.

A match made in heaven never to be broken.
Be glad and be grateful for having each other.
There's no other like her; I love you with all my life.
God, I thank you every day for your gift of a lifetime.

ARISE WITH ME, LET'S UNITE AS A NATION

When she came to you for help, what did you do?
She was talking about her children; so much drama.
I wondered where their father was; why all these issues?
You mean fathers, they're all different—I don't know.
Are you going to help or what, looking dumbfounded?

I will think about it, for how long now—I'm still thinking.
A convenient truth to get away, but nothing to think about,
Because it is not my problem; I don't understand her.
Seven children by seven different men, how possible?
Our freedom and liberty caused that; no, I don't understand.

We said, let's separate them, and destroy the families.
We found new truth in promoting individuality, it's just me.
Unity is strength but divided we will conquer them; they'll fall.
They will be marking time where we keep them while we run.
Our plan failed our children; now we're paying for it.

What do we do to reverse this anomaly; can we save them?
If we save them, can we save ourselves and our children?
Did we sell our children's souls when we sold our own?
No! We didn't, the sins of parents shall not be upon their kids.
Because they believe in one who dies for all; every belief's alike.

Oh compatriots! Arise with me, let's unite together as a nation.
We shall build an army of one, indivisible and indefatigable,
To tackle the challenges of our time; carrying each other up
As we engage in difficult conversations, tasks, and duties
To save ourselves from pending implosions, long postponed.

WHY? WHY?? WHY WEINSBERG???

Weinsberg, my dear friend, I am downcast.
The future of our democratic institution,
The liberty, freedom, and justice, has gone awry.
I went to get a permit for a civil project.
Surprisingly, I was asked for a kickback; I refused.
Why? Why?? Why Weinsberg, in this great nation???

Are you serious, this is not a third world nation?
How could that be, we are the yardstick.
Every nation is measured by our moral standards.
Who is that alien who treated you like that,
Not knowing the richness of our principled values,
The strength of our resolve, to protect our character.

He is not an alien; it happened twenty years ago.
Am still talking about it because each time I go there,
They are always missing my file, dragging me around
Unless I hire someone else to take care of it; they remember.
If I don't do that, I will never get anything done.
I know your story, you're not alone—that's why I shared.

THE BEAUTY OF THIS GENERATION

How courageous you all are,
that are born of this generation.
How lucky you all are in this age,
that you are not in their mentality.
How great are you whose mind is free,
from the insanity of past generations.
How wonderful are you of endless love,
free from the captivity of the ancients.
How marvelous are you that enjoy liberty,
that defends freedom, liberty, and Justice.
How rewarding is it to you all that fight not;
you are no longer prisoners of conscience.
'Cos of these, you're fulfilled; your dream is real.

We'll date whoever we want 'cos there's one human race.
We'll marry whoever we love 'cos we're color blind.
We'll study wherever we like 'cos we've one standard.
We'll work wherever we choose 'cos we're qualified.
We'll live wherever suits us 'cos we're one nation.
We'll have and raise our children anywhere we live.
We'll live our lives with anyone 'cos of our liberty.
We'll fight in defense of this nation 'cos we love her.
We'll die defending other's plights 'cos we love all.
We'll defend our freedom, liberty, and justice for all.
We'll protest to our government 'cos it's our right and duty.
We'll protect our constitution 'cos it's divinely inspired.
We'll govern ourselves well 'cos it's by, of, and for us.

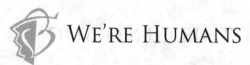 # WE'RE HUMANS

Your spouse wronged you; we're humans.
Your sibling wronged you; we're humans.
Your children wronged you; we're humans.
Your parents wronged you; we're humans.
Your associate wronged you; we're humans.
Your colleague wronged you; we're humans.
Your boss wronged you; we're humans.
Your leaders wronged you; we're humans.

Come on spouse, have you wronged someone?
Come on sibling, have you wronged someone?
Come on children, have you wronged someone?
Come on parent, have you wronged someone?
Come on associate, have you wronged someone?
Come on colleague, have you wronged someone?
Come on boss, have you wronged someone?
Come on leader, have you wronged someone?

Let's live a life of forgiveness, bearing no grudge.
Let's forgive and forget all wrongs done to us.
Let's clean our heart of all bitterness.
Let's keep no record of wrongs, bearing no malice.
Let's remember that we all sin; no one is perfect.
Let's take down the chip on our shoulders; it's heavy.
Let's avoid resentment of each other; it's all sinful.
Let's get rid of all unrighteousness; God lives in us.

OH COMPATRIOTS,
LOOK INSIDE YOU

My fellow citizens are struggling in life,
Unable to make all ends meet in life.
Those that want to go to school, can't.
They have no money to go to school.
They searched for a job but found nothing.
Those that go to school owe too much.
Those that finished school have no job.
Where is our future? Our dreams are taken.

While so much gap exists, few are doing great.
So busy chasing the worldly treasures,
Carried away by the exploit's boat,
Constantly working more than needed
To maintain a modest life of dignity.
It is truly celebrating aristocratic life,
While the majority are stuck in the turmoil.
Please be patient, hopeful, and have faith.

Oh compatriots, look inside you.
There is something you are neglecting,
Something greater than yourself.
Please wake Him up; He is alive in you.
Kick Him not to the curb, embrace Him.
Look in the mirror and you will see Him.
He is residing right inside you in waiting.
Activate Him to work for you, and all is well.

YOU ALWAYS TREAT OTHERS WELL

You always treat others well.
You are sweet at your place of work or school.
With dedication and passion,
you discharge your duties.
You go an extra mile,
for those that depend on you.
You share your life and services with them.
You love and care for them so much.
You treat all the way you want to be treated.

When you give care, you really care.
When you protect, you truly protect.
When you defend, you use all resources.
When one is in pain, you soothe.
When one suffers, you comfort.
When one lacks, you provide.
When one hurts, you heal.
When one is in jail, you visit.
When one is lost, you search.

You are not those that live for themselves,
That work for themselves and no other one.
For them, it is a reality of life to be on your own.
Everyone to their own means and survival.
They live because others can't live.
They treat others as a means to an end.
For you, others are end to a means,
For you live for the love of others.
You're like the one inside you, who loved you most.

Ever Merciful Father

Every day we pray to You.
In worship, praise, and thanksgiving
and before You, we adore in reverence.
Sometimes we fast, denying ourselves.
Yet, You seem so distant or far away.

What have we not done to You?
All which You asked us not to do
When You gave us Your command,
we disobeyed and turned our back.
Yet, You continued to watch over us.

Though we want to do what is right,
most often we end up doing what is wrong.
Help us to learn to be obedient to You.
Though we abuse your abundant grace,
Yet, You continued to abundantly bless us.

If You are far away or don't answer our call,
why should we question you for Your actions?
When we come before your presence,
looking awful and detestable in our sinfulness,
Yet, we receive so much and expect even more.

Even in Your presence, we strife with each other.
We offend, strike, hurt, and suffer one another.
We lie, deceive, cheat, steal, and envy others.
We exploit and kill one with words, mind, and body.
Yet, we expect our prayers to be answered now.

The prayers of the righteous are like a frankincense,
an aromatic offering brought before the Almighty God
with the wind tunnel blowing it into His nostrils.
In humility, our heads bowed; our knee on the ground.
Yet, some wonder why their prayer is always answered.

Oh, king Hezekiah reigned in His favor, you know.
King Solomon was blessed like never in history.
King David stole His heart; the favored apple of His eyes.
Like Abraham, in Christ, we all share in His inheritance.
Yet, there is, and will never be, anyone like Him.

YOU ARE PRINCES AND PRINCESSES

They ask, they seek, and they knock.
Anyone who asks, always receives.
Anyone who seeks, always finds.
Anyone who knocks, always enters.

Why are you always in hurry darlings?
Do you know where you are going?
You do not know where you are going.
You have no control of your life.

Humble yourself and be gentle for Him.
In love, always be tolerant to others.
Let your spirits be united in bonding.
That peace will reign among you.

Speak no evil against one another.
Uplift others with encouraging words.
Help one another and share what you have.
Love others as you love yourselves.

Redeem yourselves before God, who created you.
Let go of the spirits of anger, rage, and bitterness,
and the spirits of brawling, slander, grudge, and malice.
Grieve not the Holy Ghost in whom you're sealed.

If you do all these things above,
if you believe who you are, in who is in you,
in whose Spirit you are sealed,
you will know that you are god.

You will evoke the power of God anytime.
You will have power over all spirits.
You will have dominion over all things.
You will inherit all things that belong to God.

You Are Who God Said You Are

You are a child of God,
    you have joy.
You are the apple of His eyes,
    you have grace.
You are Him in the flesh form,
    you are very kind.
You are one of His faces,
    you are very humble.
You are made in His image and likeness,
    you are very compassionate.
You are alive because His Spirit is in you,
    you are very gentle and a living sacrifice.
You are patient, holy, and pleasing to God.

If you are His child,
    do you live like Him?
If you are the apple of His eyes,
    do you love Him?
If you are one of His form,
    how do you dress the flesh?
If you are one of His faces,
    what do you look like?
If you are His image and likeness,
    do you exemplify Him?
If His Spirit is in you,
    what do you do with it?
If you love others, you love God.

ANSWERABLE PRAYERS

Is Now syndrome, in your life?
You do not know, how to pray?
You keep asking the same thing over,
Always repeating yourself in prayers,
Saying the same prayers over and over.

Do you really know who you are talking to?
Is he deaf and dumb, like the statue gods?
Is he lame and disabled, like the heathen gods?
Is he mindless and thoughtless, like the carved gods?
No wonder why you keep asking, in repetitions.

The God I know, loves and hears me when I pray.
He is everywhere and moves wherever He wants.
He is with me everywhere because He is in me.
He knows my needs and waits on me from conception.
He watches over me and protects me from all dangers.

The God I know, is mighty and marvelous.
A wonderful God that answers by fire.
You need answers now, must have strong or big faith.
If you've little faith, lose not hope or despair, keep asking.
Please grieve not the Holy Spirit who does the work.

MY BURDENS UPON THE LORD

Oh! My mind, why do you worry so much?
Why is my soul so burdened and my body so weak?
I'll cast my worries, pains, and sufferings upon Him.
The Lord who carries them to God, our father.

Oh! My mind, why is the anxiety still so great?
My soul has no joy and my spirit is restless.
I've not cast my burdens upon the Lord.
I'm brooding over my problems all along.

Oh! My mind, harboring resentful worry, and pondering.
My soul! Embrace God's brooding, giving life and body.
My body! Receive physical manifestation over the problems
That we present to Him in our prayers.

WISDOM IS IN ALL

I found myself at the town square.
It was a town hall conference
In the city of haves and have nots,
Everyone philosophizing on issues.

I was lost among the crowds.
Statesmen from every town and city,
Local and ordinary people gathered,
Seeking, forming cohorts, and allies.

So many people have grey hair.
Great numbers dressed in gowns.
Few nobles in royal and elegant steps.
All chattering away their wisdoms.

There was one, ordinary and simple.
He was pleasing, sweet, and eloquent.
He was very young, wise, and brave.
His wisdom surpasses all grey hairs.

Even the nobles and scholars are amazed.
How marvelous, his wisdom deeply touched them.
Through his wise counsel, they found solutions.
God gives Wisdom to all ages, classes, and persons.

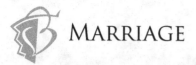

MARRIAGE

Marriage! Marriage!! What is marriage?
Husband and wife or same sex marriage?
What is the difference, are they the same?
Divine marriage and civil marriage are apart.
Husband and wife was established by God.
Same sex marriage was established by man.

Most marriages are nothing but contracts.
A business relationship between two people.
Though it starts off as love with commitment.
With terms protecting both parties' interests.
Often very selfish, dishonest, and deceptive,
Each partner hiding under a shadow.

After the knots are tied, the events start to unfold.
The one remains two, each carving out their niche.
When both kissed, their hands tightly held,
Each falling into each other's arms, warmly embraced,
It's all lies, motives, and intentions wrongly footed.
You never loved each other, you loved your flesh.

You hate each other to the point of self-destruction,
You just don't know it yet until you're tempted.
Then, you realized what a farce you are; you're a cheat,
Because everything was wrong the first day you met.
You were blinded by your shadow casting over you.
If you know it's painful, you would've done it right.

By the time you find it out, it is already too late.
That must be why most marriages last 'til death.
Divorce does not exist, separation is unheard of.
Married couples live happily ever after marriage.
Their children are never heartbroken or hurt.
They are always successful in everything they do.

In the beginning, you started off lying to each other.
You both knowingly made promises you couldn't fulfill.
You led her on to believe how much you love her.
She falls to it, doing exactly the same to you.
Like a game, you wowed each other into the deal,
Just to get into each other's carnal rousing flesh.

If you love each other, why lead each other to sin?
Your body is a temple of God, where His spirit lives.
Is He not the one who created you as man and woman
For a purposeful life with certain duty and obligation,
Divinely engineered, mastered, and planned for you?
Yet, He's mostly left out of your intentions and plans.

If He's there with you as the master planner, how could it fail?
If He's there with you, how could your sinful nature prevail?
If He has joined you together, how could you be divorced?
Only because you are disobedient to Him that created you.
You have deactivated His Holy Spirit and let in other spirits
That live in people and the environment that surrounds you.

Men and women that chose to marry one of their own sexes,
Made a deliberate choice within their free will given by God
To disobey God's will and plan just like everyone who sins.
We all sin and that is why Christ came and preached the words.
Judge them not, instead love them and pray for mankind.
God gave the right to free will, and freedom of conscience is theirs.

Civil marriage is different from divine marriage in God's order.
Have no part in civil marriage if you chose to obey God's order.
Disparage not those who choose otherwise but share the truth.
Let no one legislate morality by limiting God given freedom.
The truth has been revealed and the path set straight ahead.
It's up to mankind to choose which path to follow, in God or Satan.

WHO DO YOU THINK YOU ARE?

Who do you think you are, you mortal?
That walks around like the king of the Earth.
You think you built that by your strength.
By your power alone, that was made possible.
Through your power you can control others.
With commanding presence, you steer their lives.
If only you know the truth, you will see the true world.
You will see that your world is right at your nose.
It is neither by your personality nor by your skills.
It's not through your contact, surely not by your efforts.
As educated as you are, your knowledge is limited.
Your ability to build that depends on God inside you.
Though you're in denial, you will soon find out
How powerless, clueless, and illiterate you are
When you lie on your sick or deathbed seeking for meaning.

 # OH, LITTLE BROTHER

The journey of life became tough for him.
Early in life he smelled and felt the sting of death.
He was very young when his father was assassinated.
Now, he is old enough to understand his trail.

Oh, little bro, I can imagine what you've been through,
Left in the hands of those in whom you've trusted,
Betrayed by those you've known and loved all your life,
Handed over to strangers to be hanged by their noose.

Oh, little brother, remember who you were.
You have become a stranger to your friends and family,
Acting out and taking it out on those who truly love you,
Shutting them out and kicking them out of your life.

How did you become so mean and treacherous?
Why is your heart so dark like the color of your skin?
Why does your mouth smell like skunk to your family,
And your tongue sting like a bee to those who love you?

To strangers, you smell like roses from a thorn-full stem.
Like a flower you blossom in the wild, brightening every eye.
What is it that they've done to you? What are you running from?
Why are you so blindfolded, or is it just selective blindness?

Oh, brother, if you continue disrespecting or disobeying us,
what about the elders, parents, and superiors at work?
When will you stop disobeying the laws and authorities?
Does the Constitution, rules and regulations, mean anything?

What of the rights and freedom of those you're bullying?
Same thing you've been doing on social media, school, and work,
Not minding whose life you've taken or destroyed.
To get what you want you shoot, smash, and pulp their heads.

You steal, you cheat, and you blackmail anyone on your path.
In exchange for your freedom, you bear false witnesses.
You slander, you gossip, and you lie in framing the innocents,
All in the name of jealousness, enviousness, and greediness.

Why have you given your soul to the devil? Oh satanic agent,
I come to you today as a brother, because I love you so much.
Like a messenger of good news, you can still be saved today.
All I ask is for you to please accept Jesus Christ and be saved.

 # LOVE

Love! Oh Love!! Oh Love Divine!!!
How wonderful you are.
You are the most important gift of heaven.
You came down and gave yourself to me,
That I may enjoy life in abundance.

So, what do I give back in return for this gift?
Give to others what you gave me, that's easy!
But how? I am not pretty, intelligent, and wise,
And all these great characteristics I see in you.
Look at you: sparkling, silky, rosy, and scented.

Oh my goodness, you are so patient.
So kind, so faithful, and so low tempered.
Hey, before I forget, you are so cool,
And not proud, not rude, and definitely not selfish.
You neither envy nor boast and are not easily angered.

You've never kept record of what I've done to you.
You've never enjoyed the sensing of evils done to others.
You've always rejoiced and celebrated the truth.
You've always protected me from all evil attacks.
You've always trusted me and are always hopeful.

You give me hope because you always persevere.
You increase my faith because you've never failed.
Even with all the prophesies, you stuck with me.
My neighbor, friends, and family gossip about me,
And you are still here with me, instead of living.

As much knowledge as I show off, you argued not.
I did things to turn you off, but you loved me more.
I didn't pay back to you love for love; you're with me.
You're so pure, that you've never sinned against me.
You've never lead me to violate my person or another's.

These characteristics you've shown me are divine.
Only God has what you have; the truth is, you're god.
If I could be like you and follow your footsteps,
If I'm putting to practice what you've shown me now,
Then I'm sure that I'm giving back what you gave me.

FURNISHINGS INSIDE THE CHURCH

He was meditatively writing, as he usually does,
On the application in a Christian life:
The nature and characteristics of God
That often seem to conflict with reality.
It was four thirty in the morning, now exhausted.
He was led to sleep, then awakened at seven thirty a.m.,
An inquisition over who chooses the fabric color.
Couldn't see the urgency or emergent nature.

Understanding the need for answers to bugs in minds,
Response was that some people selected different colors,
but it was resolved at a meeting where members picked Ascot,
Has three different color schemes like red,
spot-like off-pale-white, and light grey to color coordinate.
Their selection was a good choice and had fashion sense.
People will always have a different choice on anything,
because their perceptions are as different as their faces.

What are their fashion or interior decoration skills?
Knowledge, or sense of fashion, of those inquisitors?
Their idea is that it is not grey as the carpet already is;
Take the remaining carpet and throw it over some chairs!
What is the color contrast within their own eyes?
Is it monotonous and absorbed, without color separation?
There are other furnishings inside the church.
Many more are yet to be purchased; will they match?

Decoration and furnishing are a personal thing, and style
should reflect the owner's comfort, pleasure, and essence.
The comfort, pleasure, and essence of the owner.
The Church color schemes expressed by the Overseer.
It is a known doctrine of the congregation from the beginning.
Home decoration and furnishing are quite different in style;
commercial furnishing style is usually formal and simple,
always in contrast, matched and colorfully coordinated.

Some rely so much on human thoughts,
reasoning, words, and actions as supra.
Surrendering oneself to sensuality is
contradictory to the life based on the truth,
thoughts, reasoning, mind, and actions of Christ.
Learning to master the ability to depend
solely on God in thoughts, reasoning, words, and actions,
if we say we are Christians and Christ lives in us.

With the spirit of God, then, we should get out
Of human nature and take the nature of God in us,
in our thoughts, reasoning, words, and actions.
In Matthew eighteen; twenty, Christ assured us that
"[f]or where two or three come together in my name,
there am I with them[.]" the purpose of their gathering
that fateful day was to select the color of the fabric
for the chairs that will be placed in the house of God.

They believe they gathered in God's name
And they meditatively discussed all the choices.
Then, decided that Ascot is what they wanted.
Now they are questioning the choice-making
as if God had nothing to do with their thoughts,
words, and actions regarding His house? See Exodus 25-30
Who wants to be part of such inquiry, certainly not me.
There's no more doubt whether the chairs are coming.

Or whether they will arrive before the contractor leaves;
apparently he is still there and has more work to do.
Let's not dwell on the negative, rather celebrate
the provisions of God for His place of worship.
Our God is not God of confusion, His peace reigns.
When he hands things over to Him, he let Him take charge.
He never goes back to it or questions the outcome
because no one or spirit can take away from God.

What the Lord has established, no matter how much there is,
deceit, delays, or distraction you encounter can't stop it.
God will always prevail once we allow Him to be in control.
Can you be gentle and calm in your mind, body, and spirit?
Approach others with kindness, compassion, and humility.
Be assured that you will always prevail in all that matters,
To bring glory, honor, praise, worship, and reverence to Him,
Because He is just, righteous, and generous in His blessings.

SALVATION OF A FAMILY

He speaks with a humble voice,
A gentler mumble, muttered to all.
If you are able to listen, save yourself.
It is, nonetheless, for your everlasting joy.

A personal decision to make of all choices,
To obey or disobey the inner gentle voice.
Chasing after the wind blowing all over,
Without surety of where you're going.

At dawn and dusk, you will be asked,
Checking in to account for your breadth,
What a divine duty you owed to each other.
Sacred oath taken to rear your children.

Spare not the rod nor smitten to death.
Married is one and must no longer be two.
Both man and woman are inseparable.
Your thoughts, words, and actions are one.

In His thoughts, words, and consciousness,
Everything husband and wife are doing
Are done by them as one person—Binity.
Don't think, but seek out who that Eve or Adam is.

Don't be fooled, religion can't save anyone.
Superficial exercises of the body and mind,
That warms up the spirit in preparation,
Transforms one into the supernatural and eternity.

You are very religious, but very unspiritual.
May be very spiritual, but non-religious.
What controls your thoughts, words, and actions,
yourself, your spirit, which spirit, and any conflict?

Let yourself go, kill carnality of body, mind, and soul.
Let the spirit of God take control of your life.
The executor and trustee of your body, mind, and soul.
The guarantor and insurance protection of salvation.

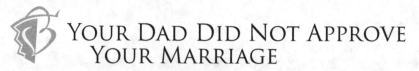

YOUR DAD DID NOT APPROVE YOUR MARRIAGE

What is wrong my darling princess?
What aches your heart my love?
Why are you so heavily laddered?
Your dad didn't approve your marriage to John.

Come closer dear, I want to tell you something.
I shared with you the story of my life.
I overheard you and your father arguing.
Please don't be destructed or hate him; my darling.

He meant well for you because he loves you so much.
You cannot marry a person because of looks.
Wealth and material possessions are not everything.
Personal potential and family values are very crucial.

Social, economic, and political status is ideal but untrue.
He is mentally and physically great but what of
His intrinsic values and moral character?
Did you pray to see if he is your Adam?

I want you to think of my stories to you.
Think about Adam and Eve out of Eden.
If all those statuses are stripped from him,
Where will you be? Remember my stories darling!

Marriage is not just a contract, there's more to it.
Pray my little angel; pray hard, it's not a joke.
Marriage is not doing what others are doing.
It is not just a responsibility due at certain age.

It is a consummate and committed mutual duty,
A very huge lifetime debt you owe to yourself.
It can be a painstaking and miserable activity.
Only God and true love sweetens everything.

Will your body, mind, and soul become one?
Body, mind, and soul belong to each other.
They become fused and inseparable from the other,
Forming a homogenous and harmonious new form.

Thessy! Only God has the power to form such union.
Such true love comes from the true love we have for God.
Share the same true love, belief, faith, trust, and hope in God.
His masterful craftsmanship recreates two into one with Christ.

My daughter, I will leave you to meditate on these words.
It's enough to take your mind off your father,
And focus on yourself. Please let me know your decision.
We're one family and together we break through all things.

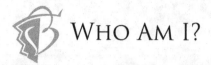

WHO AM I?

They never ask questions, what if?
And if that, what else, and who is?
They asked questions, who is, and if what?
Who am I, they defined me, and can I define me?

Look!—Inside them, their inner being.
Did you find it?—Their personal character.
The image and likeness of Him in them.
He breathed inside them and gave them life.

There are imprints, His mark—yeah, the Seal.
They have Freewill, His nature, and Spirit.
Where are the signs, blessings, and proof?
Where are the love, the power, and the control?

Who are their sources: the Father, Son, and Spirit?
They surrendered their personal sovereignty.
To who? To that one! No, the dark one,
And that one, that spirit, and that thing.

No wonder! That's why!! That's the cause!!!
Easy life always! No skin pains and no heartaches.
It's their world; diamond spoon in their mouth,
Right there on the high stools they sit.

Be fruitful and increase in number,
fill the Earth and subdue it: rule over it.
They don't understand, don't know who they are.
Very many people don't know who they are.

First, they looked inside themselves,
Deep, deep inside their inner being,
To seek out those personal characteristics,
Those that look like God: their creator.

Look in the mirror and see His image.
He is right there, like the image you saw.
He breathed His life inside them, His free will.
They can't see Him in them; they are dead.

Look at them, they think they are in charge.
I am in charge, they just don't know it yet.
Let challenges or dangers come, you'll see
How many will still be standing, on the last day.

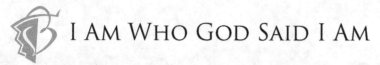

I Am Who God Said I Am

You heard them come very quietly in your life.
They said that they love you so dearly.
Very good plans have been made for you.
Now that you let them in, they took over.

No longer in control, they are in charge.
Because you let them in, they took over.
It's temporary until you know who you are,
Until you activate the power of I Am in you.

If you let them in, you lose, Him deactivated.
You drank milk as a child, now eat real food.
The word is the food, water, body, and the blood.
If you ingest and digest, it becomes the sword.

The sword and the spirit become the weapon.
Armornized and weaponized, you are ready.
The war of the physical and spirituals to be won,
Because you rejected them, you took over.

They're no longer in control, you're in charge
Because you know the right from the wrong.
You're conscious of your conscience and imagination.
You now see what God sees, creators like God.

You are co-creators in His image and likeness.
See how you represented Him to others and your milieu.
Your offspring, nurture, and creativity we could feel;
The wisdom and the power to manifest the things of God.

It can only be according to the level of the presence of God;
The grace, the fruit, and the Spirit according to His will.
Please find I am, say I am sorry, and claim to be anew.
By so doing, guide yourself and others who are lost to Him.

Be enlightened and aware of your potential
To create presently what your mind had imagined,
To be defined by your ability to discern your own uniqueness,
To make amends where, when, and very necessary.

With your personal, moral, and ethical guidelines,
You will joyously bring to their physical manifestation
That of imagination, vision, potential, discernment, uniqueness,
In the likeness of God, in whose image you were created.

DISCERNING WHO YOU ARE

Oh! Oh, son of man, from whom did you come?
From whom did you acquire the wisdom and power to create?
Because you're in touch with your inner being,
And your imagination, vision, potential, and mind,
You can create who you plan to be in the future.

Through your God-mind, you can touch them,
Physical manifestation of those intangible things;
Imagination, vision, potential, discernment, uniqueness:
It is there, in your day to day living and activities.
It is who you created, who you are, and who God is.

Every waking day is a blessing, a gift from God.
Else, are you certain of what happens in your sleep?
Your spirit is the only one very certain of who you created.
You created who you want others to see or who you are?
The same person created in the image and likeness of God?

Yes! You!! Does God reside in you and you reside in God?
What race is God, who is His enemy, what is His status?
If your spirit can testify that you are like God, you are god.
Then you can say that I am authentic; who I should be.
I am who God needs me to be and this is who I am.

THE PRODIGAL SON

God is light and because of that, you are light too.
Because you are created in His image, your light shines.
Through your light, others around you will see.
Where you stand, darkness disappears, a beacon light.
You're a guide for the ship, in voyage back to the creator.

Filled with much wisdom and power of imagination.
Filled with much vision, potential, and creative mind.
Gifts of God as He wills it, in your life, uniquely separated.
Seek to find out if that is enough to bring their physicality.
If not, willing to co-create, to cause physical manifestation?

If not, you opted out of God's family, opened yourself up
To be tempted, to be carried away, and to waste your life.
If you are humble enough to recognize your limitations,
To accept the level of God's presence in your life,
To see if you can join with another to attain fulfillment,

You will achieve self-actualization wherever you are,
in whatever you are doing or whatever is your need.
It's already yours; you're quite close to defining who you are.
If this is not the case, you are still on a journey to find yourself,
a journey to find God that is in you and should be living inside you.

Then, you are not who God created you to be.
You can use the same free will God gave you
to find yourself or rediscover yourself,
and go back to who you really are and
therefore back to God's family and Kingdom.

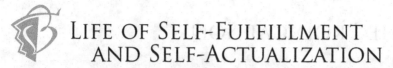

LIFE OF SELF-FULFILLMENT AND SELF-ACTUALIZATION

If you don't define yourself, someone will do so for you.
Defining and being aware of who you are is critical.
It requires self-management, being who you are.
It requires integrity, the ability to manage yourself.
It requires being in the right place in your life, with God.

It means aligning yourself with your real and truthful self.
It could also reveal that the person you are right now is unreal.
It means you may not be who you really and truly are.
It means you may be someone else, apart from who you are.
It means you have deviated from who God created you to be.

It means everything starts to fall out of place and order.
That is why self-management is inevitable.
Everything falling out of place and order in your truthful life,
Doesn't mean falling out of love and favor of God.
It means that it could also be part of that good order.

Divine order ushering in self-fulfillment and self-actualization
Shall Understand how to discern each situation and event.
It means that discernment is part of self-management,
Without which there'll be problems with self-management.
There will be a severe problem without self-management.

Oh, Discernment! Though simple, but complex.
One's ability to tune into God's wisdom
or be in tune with the wisdom of God.
Wisdom that comes from His words, written in the scriptures.
That which He whispers to us in whatever form He chooses.

Discernment is our ability to perceive
and communicate with Him in those forms He chooses;
it is not tuning into our own wisdom
or being in tune with our carnal and human self.
It is not a gut feeling, a cliché, or crystal ball.

Discernment does not come from what we said.
It doesn't come from what we did, thought, imagined, and created,
Unless it is in the image and likeness of God, in tune with His words.
That means it is truly coming from God and not humanly manipulated.
Then you will truly enjoy self-fulfillment and self-actualization.

Self-management is easy and effective if properly executed,
if you make decisions based on proper discernment and live by it.
It requires you to follow through with the program,
Propelled by your free will, with core principled value, and support.
To live like your life depends on it, like you can't do without it.

DISCERNMENT RULES

No one who wishes to listen to the radio
Or watch television tunes into his/her thoughts.
Does one tune into one's imaginations or memories?
We really and truly tune into radio or television.
We surely do not tune into songs and information in our heads
and expect to hear what the radio is broadcasting,
or see what the television or computer is showing,
unless the person is of an unsound mind.

You cannot carry out what is in your head,
and believe that you just heard it on the radio
or saw it on television, unless you are of unsound mind.
The radio or television must be turned on and tuned in to
in order to receive any communication from them.
You always turn on your phone to dial a number.
If you wish to call someone, you dial, wait for a response,
Then talk in turn to each other, waiting and listening.

Because you need to hear and understand each other,
You wait patiently for each other to speak.
You listen actively to each other's speech.
This is the same way we should turn on, tune in to,
or dial into God in order to hear and understand Him.
Discernment requires discipline. Carrying out God's will,
It requires obedience, discipleship to a belief.
It requires discipleship to the Decalogue; to the law.

It requires discipleship to moral values and ethics,
It requires discipleship to something greater than you.
You are a follower of your own core values and their sources.
You need to have the free will and the integrity
to make your feelings, your impulses, and your moods
all subordinate to those values, to His will and glory.
If you effectively and efficiently manage yourself,
your discipline comes from within, and not from outside.

The extent to which you have developed
and applied your free will in your everyday life
is measured by your personal integrity and character,
by the value you place on yourself and others.
That is what secures, stabilizes, and guarantees who you are.
It's your ability to make and keep commitments to yourself and others,
to "walk your talk" and not "talk your walk."
To love others as you love yourself and love God.

For a self-fulfilled and self-actualized person,
It means that he or she must be subordinate
to the strength, the means, and tools of the purpose.
Such subordination requires a purpose, a set mission.
It requires a clear sense of direction and value.
It requires a burning "yes" inside that makes it possible
to say "no" to other things that negate such purpose and mission.
It requires a clear sense of direction, and values—that comes from God.

It is honoring yourself, and above all God.
It is selfless given of self to I Am.
It is an offering of whole sacrifice to I Am.
It is bringing glory and honor to I Am.
It is offering your mind, body, and soul to I Am.
It is loving yourself more and more as I Am.
It is I Am loving you more and more than ever.
It is who you are; I Am is His name.

 WE ALWAYS BLAME EVERY PROBLEM IN OUR LIFE ON HIM

He already knew our thoughts and our heart,
Need not do anything to win us over,
Did not do the things He did to win us over.
Naturally being a loving Father, providing for His children,
Yet we grumble and complain for everything we dislike.
We always blame every problem in our life on Him,
Even though we are responsible for most of our problems.

The one who took the liberty to fight against us,
Has always built a large arsenal to steal our liberty.
Attacks are planned and staged on every corner of our life,
At every inch we provide for his foothold, even at childhood.
Unjust laws are made by him and just laws we do not obey.
The one, who lays a blockade, lays ambush for us,
To prevent us from getting close to Him who made us.

Right from our childhood, he steers us away from purity,
Knowing how playful we are and how much we learn playing,
When we copy and mimic all perceptions and sensualities,
Presented with the beauty, corrupting, and enticing influences.
We lose perception of natural, Godly, and human laws,
In the way we engage or promote physical or cultural activities
And social and emotional development of one another.

How we prevent criminal activities and justice systems
Determines how enhanced and functional our families are.
Families and individuals empowered to increase and abound
In their own economic independence and productivity,
and strong, healthy, supportive communities, and society
that have a positive impact on the quality of life
and the development of children, adolescents, youth, and families.

THEY ARE FUSSING GOD OUT

What is that fussing all about?
That they are blessed with great abundance,
Having made so much progress in this world,
Greatly advanced in things they can do or make,
To the extent that, they are fussing God out.
They forced God out of public life and arena.
Where did all those achievements come from?

My Children, what is that bickering among you about?
They are forcing God out of their personal life.
They abdicated their primary responsibility
To bring up their children in fear of God.
They stopped teaching them to live in the Spirit.
Look at the different problems and issues they have now.
Look at the painful process of achieving their dreams.

They are teaching them to live on the flesh, and now.
They live by the moment and think not of the future.
The search for God's image and likeness in them waned,
And the prospects for future community outreach is dying.
The days of the frontiers seem so long gone,
But it was just yesterday, in comparison with world events.
They gave us a voice, now the voice is going, going, gone.

Who usurped the voice of the people but the highest bidder?
Are there alternative ways of achieving these missions?
The struggles, trials, tribulations, sufferings, and the stress.
Why is one person or community preferred over another?
Don't we share the same burden and the same cause?
Don't we share the same course and the same objective?
Don't we share the same goals and desire the same outcome?

For our community, our state and our nation, everyone is needed!
We are supposed to complement one another,
Always thinking and knowing the truth,
Though everyone can't be satisfied.
We can't make everyone happy, but we should try.
It is the fulfillment of the will of our Founding Fathers,
Expressed in the Declaration of Independence.

"We hold these truths to be self-evident,
that all men are created equal,
that they are endowed by their Creator
with certain unalienable rights,
that among these are life, liberty
and the pursuit of happiness."
Anything to the contrary violates that truth.

It is the right thing to do my children.
If you make people unhappy, you will not be happy.
John is unhappy and makes Jane unhappy.
Jane in return makes John very unhappy.
Such comes from vengeance and unforgiving spirit.
Our lives will be better if we avoid making others unhappy.
Even if they make us unhappy, make them happy.

SAVE US FROM THE BEASTS AND MONSTERS WE HAVE CREATED

The rules and regulations are good if justified.
A stifling and hanging noose around our neck,
With power to tighten it, in the hands of very few.
People that know how to make nothing but spending,
Distributing our wealth among ourselves and friends.

Where is the oversight, where is the accountability?
Where are the employers, the people, and the taxpayers?
Servants of the people, have become their masters.
Lords and kings over the people, doing what we revolted for.
They use the people to leverage themselves and get ahead.

The people keep giving, giving a little, a lot, and too much.
When are the people going to get back their shares?
A return to their investment: life security and stability!
Please do something, to our infrastructure, and future.
Shore up our foundation around our small businesses.

The source of our sustenance and subsistence is going.
Feed our main streets, so that we can get to the beltway,
Then to the wall streets, broad streets, and the skyways.
Integrate our communities and stimulate our lives.
Look at our social, recreational, and interpersonal lives.

We fuss, harm, curse, fight, and kill each other,
Because we are sad, sick, helpless, hopeless, and angry.
The well-being of our mind, body, and soul is gone.
Also that of our dreams, economy, politics, and spirit.
Please give us protection: self-help, safe streets, and home.

Give us chances to achieve our dreams and happiness.
Give us chances to live our dreams and self-fulfilled life.
Have mercy, spare our lives from the wolves and the lions.
Save us from the beasts and monsters we have created
From the balloons our silence created to be gods over us.

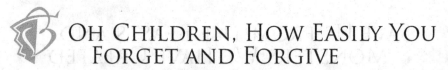

OH CHILDREN, HOW EASILY YOU FORGET AND FORGIVE

We gather, to play, to fuss, and to fight.
We're ready to forgive, to make up, and to play.
We walk, we chase, we run, and with troves.
We trope, we jive, we obey, and we rebel.

So eager to write on our blank and clean slate.
Seeking answers to all possible questions.
Our curiosity and thirst for knowledge to quench
Insatiable urges and impulses to control.

Though young and fearless, we boldly test
The barriers, boundaries, and our space,
As we share every bit of information learned,
As we play, fuss, fight, love, and like each other.

Oh children, how easily you forget and forgive.
This minute you're mad, next you're happy,
Now you're crying, next you're laughing,
In a moment you're fighting, later you're playing.

What can I do to guarantee your safety?
What can I do to plan for your future?
How can I guard your crossing of the roads,
With all these stumbling blocks in your path?

Walking in droves across to the parks,
In droves you skate and bike to the playground,
Surrounded by emptiness and risk of death,
Nothing to stimulate your experiences or challenge you.

What chances to grow without dangers in your face?
What chances to go to school without being bullied?
What chances to grow, to work, and fully develop?
What chances to avoid the gangs and peer pressure?

Can you grow without testing those liquors?
Can you grow without snuffing and puffing?
Can you grow without inhaling, and say no to drugs?
Those dangerous substances that we metamorphose.

We have doomed your days, nights, and dreams,
With greed and gluttony in the shows, games, and movies
Our corrupting influences secretly designed.
Packages delivered to the advantage of your vulnerability.

We are sorry that many have sold their soul to the devil
by exposing you to so much struggle, leaving you no legacy,
Leaving you vulnerable, unprotected, and without future.
Growing up is a curse; a challenge; a burden to the grave.

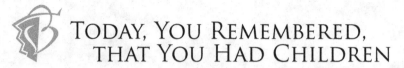

TODAY, YOU REMEMBERED, THAT YOU HAD CHILDREN

Today, you remembered, that you had children.
What have you done for me mother?
What have you done for me father?
Every day you complain about me.
You talk about me worse than your enemies.
You call me names worse than your dogs.

If I am not useless, I will become a criminal.
If my sister is not a slut, I will become a convicted felon.
Everything is my fault or my sister's failures.
Where were you, when I was little?
Where were you, when my sister was raped?
Where were you, when I was beaten and bullied?

You were always gone, far away from our life,
Always at work or hanging out with your friends.
It was Joe this, It was Joe that,
It was Sylva this, and it was Sylva that.
Always on a cruise or traveling around the globe.
Always in a fight when your baby's father is at home.

We couldn't call him our daddy; he was never around.
Always going to one party or another fun' raising.
Always in the street, always in a club, all's about you.
When you're at home, your face is buried in your work.
We're dumped at the day care centers and picked up late.
We're raised by our nanny, who was very fond of her children.

Where were you, when we graduated from primary school?
Where were you, when we graduated from middle school?
Where were you, when we graduated from high school?
What color were our school uniforms, mother and daddy?
What color were our school team uniforms?
Which college did we attend and what did we study?

How many PTA meetings did you attend?
Were you there to share me up during any of my games?
Did any of you help with any of our homework?
You always throw it in our face how you paid the bills.
You brag about all the expensive clothing and apparels.
You throw money at us, when we run to hug you.

Do you know what your rejection did to our self-worth?
Who told you we cared about any of those gifts?
We needed our parents to be at our games like others.
Attend PTA meetings, our games, and graduations like others.
Other kids talked about their mothers washing their clothes.
Mother, you never did; it was nanny, babysitter, and all strangers.

We wanted you to drive us to school, just like our friends.
We wanted you to hold our hands when we walked the park.
We wanted you to play with us when we played football games.
We wanted you to take us to practice, lessons, and movies.
We wanted to be held, hugged, and kissed when we tripped.
You abandoned us to strangers, hurrying to go home to their children.

We were moved from home to home while you and dad fought.
You staged a battle over who owns the pieces of properties.
Those properties are us; today you blame us for worthlessness.
Daddy, mommy, today is our first thanksgiving together.
Today, you remembered, that you had children.
You expect us to be excited to see you at grandpas.

Today, you met us here, and you want to be our parents,
Thirty years after you abandoned us to our fate,
Now that you are weakened by your old age and resources,
Loudly you complain about what your money purchased for you.
We forgave you, that we may prosper, and cherish our blessings.
We pray that God will forgive you and may He bless both of you.

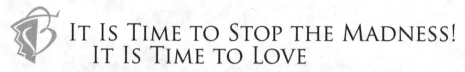

IT IS TIME TO STOP THE MADNESS! IT IS TIME TO LOVE

I ran into a buddy. He says to me, "Hey, buddy! What's up?"
I responded back, "Nothing much! Same old, same old story!"
Then, we slapped our palms together
And grasped each other's hands.
We hugged each other, our hearts pressed against each other,
Our other hands against each other's backs.
Then we bounced apart, strengthened by the warmth we felt.
Again we balled our fists together as one.
Holding one fist against the other, we freed our hands,
snapping our fingers—but instead of letting go,
we ball our fists again in reassurance;
one gently bumping on the top
and then the bottom of the other.
Then we pump power into each other's balled fists;
a kiss of life and strength, reminding each other
of how far we have come together.

Finally, we thrust two fingers up into the air,
then hold them across our chests as a sign of peace among us.
In such an act of loyalty, hope, and faithfulness,
I see a theatrical performance of our agreement with one another,
Between us and God; I see the warmness of one heart,
that is fond of another, that cares and loves.
I see encouragement, empowerment, and support.
I see a hole at the end of the tunnel and I have light in my hand.
I feel the blood flowing hard in my veins, heart pumping hard.
I feel the chills, the air letting out of my lungs, and the sweat.
I feel the breeze from the ocean, bringing my dream to reality.
I see a reminder of our history, a vigorous invigoration.
I see recommitment and reaffirmation of who we are as a people
each time we see each other and repeat the same act.
Why, then, do we kill each other over nothingness?
It is time to stop the madness! It is time to love!

 Do Not Take Them Out of the World, Protect Them

You are who He said you are, no one can change that.
You are who you said you are, if you know the truth.
His word will never return to Him, without being fulfilled.
There is nothing anyone or spirit can do to you
Unless you permit it, agree to it, and set the stage.

He has blessed you forever, even before you were born.
His gift has been scattered all over, for those who seek Him.
He that supplies seed to the sower, also supplies bread.
He has increased your seed store, your harvest abounds.
You'll embrace Him, through whom all your blessings come.

Do not boast of man, because you know whom your source is.
His divine power, has given us all we need in life.
That through them, you will participate in divine nature.
Ask, seek, and knock, that you will receive, find, and enter.
Call to Him, He will answer you, and reveal his will to you.

MONO-RACISM

Anger always arouses and serious uprising starts
Over racism between one race and another.
But we ignore or express no interest
if it is between and among the same race.
Racism set not to occur between the same people.
I think it does, if you judge others racially.
Defiling thoughts, words, and actions
In prejudicial conduct, engaged by any
Thoughts, words, and acts due to race.
Though they mistreat one another due to race,
They believe that they're superior to another.
Even a brown skin black mistreating a dark skin black,
An English white mistreating an Irish white.
Anglo-Saxon or Anglo-Celtic matters not here.
Such prejudice avails racism
To those of the same race or colors.
Regardless of similarities, such is evil.
Mono-racism ignored to damn the same people.
Pure discrimination hiding in a blind spot.
Their victims lay in states of biases
Caused by those dishing out injustice,
As their voices silently cry out to us
To protect them like victims by other races
As protection equal before the law.

A Culture of Injustice, Quiet and Undignified

Get rid of that, get rid of that!
Those mundane actions and thinking processes,
A culture of injustices, quiet and undignified,
Hanging as wedges, tied to our civilization,
Mono-racism and multi-racism being the same.

Rights, liberty, justice, and freedom differently granted.
God given rights, now are, entitlements indifferently deprived.
Investigation rarely conducted of these breaches.
What a robbery of people's properties;
Worth the protection of pupils' probity.

They need no rubber ring or Band-Aids of it surfaces.
Taken from the people without due process,
Because he said, because she said.
Whistle blown by lying tongues,
Quickened by judgment, conclusively assumed.

In the name of law, rules and regulations,
Transparency, accountability, and responsibilities.
Our values, morals, and principles entrapment
In the rush to make history or news for our glory.
Some destroy the principles and its core values

You Bureaucrats, the People's Servants

You bureaucrats, the people's servants,
Dare not interfere, but promote our values.
Do not assault our free market enterprise,
The epicenter of our existence as a nation.
Epicritic to fulfillment of our dreams,
The dreams of our fathers and founders.

You bureaucrats, the people's servants,
Protect our thin fibered small businesses,
Protect our future, our children's future.
Probable cause, good faith, is not all?
Give us a break! Please verify hearsay.
Validate, authenticate, and substantiate.

Beware of the disgruntled elements,
Enemies of our free market economy.
Beware of the false earthquake-like attack.
Beware of its aftershock to our businesses.
Beware of the crumbling of its structures.
Beware of those the debris collapses over.

Beware of your powers and authorities.
Beware of your immunities from prosecution.
The good of principality and superiority
is that of awareness, to use it to protect others
And never to use it to abuse or suppress others.
Beware of the pains, sufferings, costs, and damages.

How Unjust and Destructive Some Principalities Are

How unjust and destructive some principalities are.
The power of interference in our lives and dreams
That creates malicious prosecution at the will of our servants.
Malicious use of criminal proceedings against the ruled;
malicious use of judicial proceedings and vicarious liability;
persons aiding or abetting, in the persecutions and prosecutions;
and all forms of interference with economic or business relationships.

How unjust and destructive some principalities are.
The power that causes interference within our rights
And liberty to pursue: business, trade, or occupation;
institution or continuation of judicial proceedings;
the malicious use of process and abuse of process;
and violations of several fundamental rights of our people.
The people who are their employer, whom they are serving.

Both human and corporate individuals are overburdened
With proceedings too expensive to litigate and win
by average individuals with shallow pockets and subsistence.
It takes with it, the individual's dignity and limited resources.
Our people are often forced out or they give up.
Their victimization will continue until we provide them a safety net
which will stimulate more people to venture out and be creative.

 BINITY

The man came unto a woman
Face-to-face and they fused together.
Mind-to-mind, body-to-body,
Spirit-to-spirit, they joined together.

Binary fission—one person created by God,
Divided equally by circumstances of their birth,
Eagerly searching for each other's half,
later found each other, and reunited as one.

Some people call it soulmate.
Never reunite with the wrong part—individual.
You are doomed if you heed not,
A marriage abounding in severe conflicts.

Compared to the rejection reactions
common to the human body part transplants,
requiring several scientific tests and drugs
to ensure that they match and prevent rejection.

Individuals who find their other half
Should subject themselves to testing.
Test the mind, body, and soul to match.
Use divine spirit of discernment in the testing.

Seek the divine truth to validate the one.
Match with yourself for authentication.
Before you join together, remember Love and trust.
Love seals the cracks in the joints of the two parts as one.

The marital conflicts from any mismatch results to:
Lack of homogeneous unity, harmony, and balance
in the coexistence of both individuals as one.
They will remain divided in the body of Jesus Christ.

Reuniting with the right part of you
peacefully manifests biosis—a way of life; behaviors
And character reformations that are based on the truth
inherent in the word of God and life of our Lord Jesus Christ.

Building a strong God fearing family is
the foundation for a stronger community and
the center of the strongest society in the world.
It starts with binity—the fusing of male and female humans.

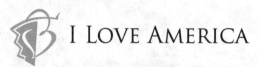

I LOVE AMERICA

I love America very much
Because God loves America.
I love America
Because America loves me too.
I love America
As much as I love myself.
I love America
Because she is founded upon the words of God.
I love America
Because she believes in God.
I love America
Because her Constitution protects all and sundry.
I love America
Because we share the same beliefs.
I love America
Because we share the same values.
I love America
Because we share the same dream.
I love America
Because I believe in her.
I love America
Because she is like me.
I truly love America
Because all things are yours that you work hard for;
knock, seek, and ask her Father Almighty.
I love the United States of America.

SPEAK UP NOW OR FOREVER REMAIN SILENT

Those children are ready and want to marry.
They need to marry to continue the lineage.
It's their life to live now, I have no input
To the things they do, and choice of their spouse; I was told.

Keep quiet, they are eighteen, and allow them to perish,
Knowing that their choices will do more harm to them.
Speak up against their choices, and be hated by them.
What choices are mine, knowing both dangers ahead?

Speak up now or forever remain silent.
Speak up now or forever remain miserable.
Speak love and kindness, to save these children.
Speak now and be saved, from eternal condemnation.

Speak later and be rewarded, with eternal damnation.
Eli spoke not to his sons, and received divine justification.
Wait not 'til it's too late to save, early intervention is profitable.
Help them be joyous, your life will be long, and you will rejoice.

THERE IS A PLACE FOR A GOOD PARENT TO START

Numbers at thirty and three to six,
There is a place for a good parent to start.
First Samuel at two and twelve to thirty six,
There is a taste for a good food to the soul.

Feed them milk, before feeding them burgers.
Rear them in the Lord, if you wish them to obey.
Love them to death, if you wish them to live.
Allow them to fly, by giving them their wings.

Getting married nowadays has become something awful.
Get married today and become divorced in three days.
Getting married as ever, has ever been great for procreation.
Where's God in all these failed marriages and lives?

Look back to Adam, Noah, and Abraham,
Isaac, Jacob, Joseph, and all God's beloved.
How graceful their married lives, were placed under God.
How preeminent His presence, were in all their marriages.

THE COVER

We deserve equipped parks where people of this nation play.
We really need group of friends always giving or receiving secondary education.
We need group of peers always giving or receiving tertiary education
We truly desire communities where people of this nation live in fulfillment

The sunlight always beaming from above
The source of food, power, and energy
Supplying life to the plants, park, garden, and the community
And the green plants and community supply power and energy to all living things.

The sunshine reminding all; of the power of God.
The daylight, secondary, and tertiary education enlighten the path to great future.
All groups of friends show crucial social behavior;
Relationships needed for all human development.

Group friendship shows care and love for each other.
The mixture of races brings unity in diversity.
Cultural differences and sensitivities leads to racial and cultural identity maturity
Without these one is incomplete and underdeveloped.

The cover signals love of yourself, family, friends, neighbors, community, and country.
The whole cover shows the way to achieve happiness and joy in life.
The way surely leads to achievements, self-fulfillment, and self-actualization.
The book designed indeed to manifests the future we all dream about.

END

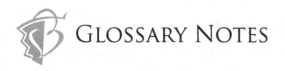

GLOSSARY NOTES

A

A Culture of Injustice, Quiet and Undignified

The author in this poem appeals to the people to do something about the injustice and conducts that undermine our values and constitution.... 148

A Friend Is the One Like You

In this poem, the poet describes what a true friend is 96

A Land of Opportunity for Dreamers of All Nations

The poet in this poem highlights the challenges of immigration, hopes, and dreams of all residents 88

Alex I Love but Smith I Hate

In this poem, the poet highlights the frustration, emotional pains, and suffering of a woman in love with a person of another race........... 82

A Little Boy Young and Restless

The author in this poem told a story of people in distress and was challenged by people more powerful; the smallest person among them came out to challenge them and won............................ 37

A Man Who Knows About a Thing

This cautions about following people who are wise and staying away from fools... 59

Answerable Prayers

This poem expresses why some prayers may not be answered and why some should. It highlights the significance of faith in prayers 110

Arise Compatriots You All Aryan Nations

In this poem, the poet captions the emotions of a white supremacist blowing the war trumpet, calling out his people to action to protect their people and power

Arise with Me, Let's Unite As a Nation

In this poem, the author highlights people discussing the trouble in our society, which was started by a wrong notion and norms that have caused severe damage to our culture, leaving a massive hole in our family and individual life. This problem can only be fixed through unity and collaboration

B

Baltimore

The poet in this poem looked at Baltimore through the lens starting at the south side through the north side, a cross section of the old city that withstood the pressures of the independent wars that established the greatest nation on Earth today

Because I Am White

In this poem, the poet explores the feelings of a particular white male regarding the way he perceives his relationship with minority races.

Beloved I Have Heard You

In this poem, the man responding to his beloved in *Love on the Noose* shares his emotions in honor of his betrothed request

Binity

In this poem, the author advises people planning to get married to be careful and discern their actions.

C

D

E

Ever Merciful Father

F

Furnishings Inside the Church

G

Give Them Life

H

How Unjust and Destructive Some Principalities Are

I

J

Jungle Kingdom

K

L

Labor in Your Dreams

Let's Work and Let's Share

Life of Self-Fulfillment and Self-Actualization

Love

Love a Distance

In this poem, the author portrays the inner character of a man of God at the moment of temptation. He received the grace of God to overcome the temptation and reconciled himself with his father.................... 44

Love on the Noose

In this poem, I try to project the image of two lovers who were planning to get married, only to find out that the woman encountered a natural disaster. Without thinking of herself or her desires, she cancelled the plan and set her fiancé free from the bondage of emotional pains and the suffering of seeing her suffering death............................ 11

Love Yourselves

The author in this poem highlights the need for people to love themselves by loving others, including the traits they need to possess to love others ... 71

M

Making a Career in that Field

This poem highlights the inner struggle between passion, sense of duty, and dedication to one's career or profession and money.............. 67

Marriage

This author delved into marriage inequality and same sex marriage ... 113

Mono-racism

The author in this poem highlights the damaging effects of actions caused by people of the same race, which if done by another race would be classified as racism; yet, nothing is done about it. The author called it Mono-racism 147

Oh Compatriots, Look Inside You

Oh, Little Brother

P

The Prodigal Son

Public Enemy

Q

R

Rewarding Relationship and Genuine Love Divine

S

The Chameleon

In this poem I discuss the life of a chameleon. Like other animals used in my poem, I highlighted its deceptive practices and lifestyle which ended up becoming a defensive mechanism to protect him from predators

The Cover

The poet in this poem, Quid pro quo, summarizes what the book is about: what we get from God in exchange for what we invest into the people and environment

The Dog Fight

This poem presents the underground life of dog fight, both for game and entertainment. It highlights the culture that promotes violence among some people and cruelty towards dogs and animal in general

The Eagles in the Sky

In this poem, the author looks at the Earth from the sky above the Earth through the eye of the eagles, discussing with the people of the Earth about their relationship in a two-way communication of charges and counter-charges responses

The Elephant

The author in this poem discusses the life, characteristics, and beauty of the elephant

The Holy Trinity Is at Work

In this poem, the author tries to make sense of God in a very succinct definition of an indefinable nor characterizeable Being

The Justice

Justice is a demand placed on mankind taking example from God. It is hard to have that expectation met when we have winners or losers in any dispute. Quite a good number are settled amicably but the only guarantee is fair trial. What is your experience? This poem looks at different challenges common in our judicial system

The Lion's Den

In this poem, the author looked at the life of intruders into the lion's den. A conversation ensued between the intruder and the lion that is the head of its household. The lion, in response to the inquisition of the intruder, made its case why he is such a feared but revered beast

The Man She Loved So Dearly

The author in this poem projected a love connection between two people who did not allow God to initiate their marriage plan experienced setback as soon it blossomed

The Town Where You Were Born

The author in this poem explores more about a woman of his dream

The Realities of Life

The poet in this poem highlights the realities of life. Our action has counter-reaction to any action

The Wasteland of Americas of Native Descents

In this poem, the poet highlights the life of a person from the native's perspective

The Usurper Is Coming

The author writes about people's experience with principalities trying to steal their dreams, and they handed them over to God who is just and righteous

Why? Why?? Why Weinsberg???

This author portrays a picture of a person being consoled by another over their world encounter with an authority figure in the first world 101

Who Do You Think You Are?

In this poem, the author highlights the emptiness and ineptitude of those who think they can do all things and are in control of anything. How could they feel that way when they cannot control the air in their lungs and have no idea when it will expire? 115

Wisdom Is in All

In this poem, the Poet points out that wisdom is God's given gift to whomever He pleases regardless of age, education, or class 112

X

Y

You Always Treat Others Well

In this poem, the author highlights the differences between two kinds of workers: a self-fulfilled and a self-centered person 105

You Are Princes and Princesses

In this poem, the poet highlights the Christian characteristics that bring the physical manifestation of God's presence and power 108

You Are the One in My Dream

The author in this poem shares that dream is one of the ways God can minister to people 48

Z

 # BIBLIOGRAPHY

1. New International Version. The Holy Bible. Japan. The Zondervan Corporation. 1987.
2. Elochukwu, Ebelechukwu. How To Win Your Trials & Your Community. Florida. Xulon Press. 2012.
3. Elochukwu, Ebelechukwu. The Lost Legacy. Texas. AuthorHouse 2012
4. New World Dictionary of the American Language. Webster's New World Dictionary. Wenatchee. William Collins + World Publishing Co. Inc. 1978.
5. www.Wikipedia.org